TARGET YOUR MATHS

Year 4

Practice Workbook

Elmwood Education

First published 2018 by
Elmwood Education
Unit 5
Mallow Park
Watchmead
Welwyn Garden City
Herts. AL7 1GX
Tel. 01707 333232

ISBN 9781 906 622 671

Typeset and illustrated by Tech-Set Ltd., Gateshead, Tyne and Wear.
Cover illustrated by Stephen Hill
Email: hilly.moto@btinternet.com
Printed and bound in Great Britain by TJ International Ltd. Padstow

PREFACE

Target your Maths Year 4 Practice Workbook has been written to accompany Target your Maths Year 4 Text Book. The Practice Workbook is intended to provide pupils with the material to consolidate their learning, whether used in the classroom or at home.

The structure of the Practice Workbook matches that of Appendix III found in Target your Maths Year 4 Answer Book. In Appendix III the Year 4 Programme of Study is organised into twelve termly blocks. In Appendix IV overleaf each page of the Practice Workbook is matched with the corresponding block and page(s) of Target your Maths Year 4 Text Book.

Whereas each lesson in Target your Maths Year 4 is pitched at three different ability levels, the Practice Workbook is based solely upon the requirements of Year 4 pupils, the ability level covered by Section B of Target your Maths.

The author is indebted to many colleagues who have assisted him in this work. He is particularly grateful to Sharon Granville and Davina Tunkel for their invaluable assistance and advice.

Stephen Pearce

APPENDIX IV

The references are for the blocks found in Appendix III of the Target your Maths Year 4 Answer Book and the page numbers in the Target your Maths Year 4 Text Book.

TERM 1		BLOCK	PAGE(S)
1	Numbers	1	2–3
2	Place Value	1	4
3	Mental +/− of Multiples of 10, 100, 1000	2	16
4	Written Method +	3	22
5	Written Method −	3	24
6	Multiplication Facts for 6	3	33
7	Equivalent Fractions	4	64
8	Reading Clocks	5	104–105
9	12-hour/24-hour Clocks	5	104–106
10	Two-dimensional Shapes	6	110–111
11	Multiplication Facts for 7	7	34
12	Written Method ×/÷ 1	7	48, 50
13	Decimal Fractions	8	73
14	Metric Units 1	8	82–84
15	Bar Charts – Presenting Data	9	124–125
16	Multiplication Facts for 9	10	35
17	Multiplying Multiples of 10/100	10	40
18	Word Problems (×/÷ Facts)	10	55
19	Area and Perimeter 1	11	92–95
20	Comparing Angles	12	118

TERM 2		BLOCK	PAGE(S)
21	Counting	1	7
22	Rounding	1	10
23	Using +/− Facts	2	15
24	Written Method +/− 1	2	23, 25
25	Multiplication Facts Review 1	3	36
26	Multiplication Facts for 11	3	37
27	Written Method ×/÷ 2	3	49, 52
28	Decimals – Money and Measures	4	76–77
29	Metric Units 2	5	85–87
30	Triangles and Quadrilaterals	6	112–113
31	Describing Positions	6	120

Year 4

CONTENTS

Write these numbers in figures.

1 three hundred and ninety-five ....

2 four thousand one hundred and forty-two ....

3 nine hundred and thirty-seven ....

4 two thousand five hundred and ten ....

5 one thousand and sixty-eight ....

6 six thousand seven hundred and four ....

7 five thousand eight hundred and seventy-one ....

8 three thousand three hundred and twenty-six ....

9 seven thousand and eighty-three ....

10 nine thousand two hundred and nine ....

Write these numbers in words. Take care with the spelling.

11 1524 ....

12 961 ....

13 7108 ....

14 9235 ....

15 5073 ....

16 2849 ....

17 8300 ....

18 6417 ....

19 3002 ....

20 9036 ....

The value of a digit depends upon its place in the number.

Example $5439 = 5000 + 400 + 30 + 9$

Write the value of the underlined digit.

1 1<u>7</u>83 ....

2 52<u>9</u>7 ....

3 <u>2</u>638 ....

4 90<u>4</u>1 ....

5 4<u>5</u>12 ....

6 <u>6</u>164 ....

7 89<u>2</u>5 ....

8 374<u>6</u> ....

9 7<u>6</u>09 ....

10 13<u>5</u>3 ....

11 <u>9</u>432 ....

12 5<u>8</u>17 ....

13 498<u>5</u> ....

14 <u>8</u>269 ....

15 25<u>7</u>8 ....

Work out

16 $7254 + 60$ ....

17 $3847 - 3000$ ....

18 $6763 + 800$ ....

19 $9329 - 90$ ....

20 $2135 + 5000$ ....

21 $8406 - 600$ ....

22 $1971 + 70$ ....

23 $5018 - 2000$ ....

24 $4692 + 400$ ....

25 $7565 - 80$ ....

Write down what needs to be added or subtracted to change:

26 3348 to 2948 ....

27 9452 to 9472 ....

28 8194 to 2194 ....

29 5737 to 5687 ....

30 8826 to 9726 ....

31 1675 to 6675 ....

32 4281 to 3581 ....

33 7952 to 8032 ....

34 5368 to 9368 ....

35 2073 to 9973 ....

Write the missing number in the box.

1 3154 + 70 = ☐

2 5827 + 600 = ☐

3 2403 + 3000 = ☐

4 ☐ + 50 = 1932

5 ☐ + 900 = 7680

6 ☐ + 4000 = 4218

7 1646 + 150 = ☐

8 5810 + 3200 = ☐

9 7257 + 420 = ☐

10 ☐ + 1700 = 8361

11 ☐ + 520 = 3199

12 ☐ + 2300 = 6732

13 5192 + 206 = ☐

14 4503 + 1004 = ☐

15 1965 + 350 = ☐

16 ☐ + 602 = 2487

17 ☐ + 2005 = 4825

18 ☐ + 3030 = 6394

19 5139 − 800 = ☐

20 7570 − 2000 = ☐

21 1625 − 90 = ☐

22 ☐ − 700 = 3943

23 ☐ − 5000 = 2218

24 ☐ − 60 = 4872

25 2435 − 1400 = ☐

26 3901 − 3500 = ☐

27 2394 − 2100 = ☐

28 ☐ − 2800 = 5166

29 ☐ − 4300 = 1280

30 ☐ − 6400 = 957

31 6775 − 1009 = ☐

32 4612 − 205 = ☐

33 9443 − 4070 = ☐

34 ☐ − 5002 = 4326

35 ☐ − 308 = 2198

36 ☐ − 2040 = 3874

> *Examples*
>
> $$\begin{array}{r} 1\ 6\ 8\ 5 \\ +\ \ \ 4\ 3\ 9 \\ \hline 2\ 1\ 2\ 4 \\ \tiny 1\ \ 1\ \ 1 \end{array} \qquad \begin{array}{r} 5\ 2\ 9\ 3 \\ +1\ 8\ 4\ 7 \\ \hline 7\ 1\ 4\ 0 \\ \tiny 1\ \ 1\ \ 1 \end{array}$$
>
> Remember to add the carried figure.

Work out

1
$$\begin{array}{r} 4\ 9\ 3\ 5 \\ +\ \ \ 5\ 4\ 8 \\ \hline \end{array}$$

2
$$\begin{array}{r} 7\ 2\ 6\ 7 \\ +\ \ \ 8\ 5\ 3 \\ \hline \end{array}$$

3
$$\begin{array}{r} 1\ 6\ 8\ 9 \\ +\ \ \ 7\ 0\ 4 \\ \hline \end{array}$$

4
$$\begin{array}{r} 5\ 8\ 4\ 6 \\ +\ \ \ 1\ 5\ 9 \\ \hline \end{array}$$

5
$$\begin{array}{r} 3\ 1\ 7\ 4 \\ +\ \ \ 6\ 5\ 8 \\ \hline \end{array}$$

6
$$\begin{array}{r} 6\ 0\ 5\ 8 \\ +\ \ \ 9\ 7\ 7 \\ \hline \end{array}$$

7
$$\begin{array}{r} 3\ 5\ 7\ 3 \\ +2\ 4\ 4\ 8 \\ \hline \end{array}$$

8
$$\begin{array}{r} 5\ 7\ 4\ 9 \\ +3\ 9\ 7\ 6 \\ \hline \end{array}$$

9
$$\begin{array}{r} 2\ 8\ 8\ 6 \\ +1\ 3\ 9\ 4 \\ \hline \end{array}$$

10
$$\begin{array}{r} 6\ 4\ 6\ 5 \\ +2\ 2\ 3\ 6 \\ \hline \end{array}$$

11
$$\begin{array}{r} 4\ 3\ 9\ 8 \\ +3\ 7\ 3\ 4 \\ \hline \end{array}$$

12
$$\begin{array}{r} 7\ 6\ 7\ 7 \\ +1\ 8\ 2\ 6 \\ \hline \end{array}$$

13
$$\begin{array}{r} 1\ 8\ 6\ 4 \\ +1\ 2\ 3\ 9 \\ \hline \end{array}$$

14
$$\begin{array}{r} 3\ 6\ 9\ 6 \\ +1\ 7\ 8\ 6 \\ \hline \end{array}$$

15
$$\begin{array}{r} 4\ 5\ 8\ 5 \\ +2\ 9\ 6\ 5 \\ \hline \end{array}$$

16
$$\begin{array}{r} 5\ 9\ 7\ 8 \\ +2\ 7\ 8\ 5 \\ \hline \end{array}$$

17
$$\begin{array}{r} 2\ 8\ 3\ 7 \\ +2\ 8\ 6\ 5 \\ \hline \end{array}$$

18
$$\begin{array}{r} 6\ 4\ 5\ 9 \\ +1\ 6\ 8\ 2 \\ \hline \end{array}$$

	2 13 1		6 11 14 1
Examples	3̷ 4̷ 6 9		7̷ 2̷ 5̷ 0
	− 1 9 7 4		− 4 6 8 3
	1 4 9 5		2 5 6 7

Work out

1   4 3 7 0
   − 1 5 2 4

2   6 4 2 9
   − 4 8 5 5

3   9 6 1 3
   − 2 4 6 8

4   7 0 8 2
   − 6 1 7 9

5   5 1 4 5
   − 3 9 5 0

6   8 7 3 6
   − 4 1 9 7

7   3 2 6 5
   − 2 6 1 7

8   5 5 4 0
   − 4 1 6 5

9   7 3 1 7
   − 3 3 5 4

10   9 1 9 3
   − 6 3 8 4

11   4 9 2 2
   − 2 3 4 7

12   6 8 3 8
   − 5 8 7 6

13   8 4 2 1
   − 2 3 8 8

14   9 5 3 6
   − 5 9 6 5

15   3 4 5 7
   − 1 9 5 9

16   6 8 1 4
   − 2 1 4 6

17   7 0 7 0
   − 5 8 3 2

18   5 3 4 9
   − 2 4 4 6

Write the missing number in the box.

1 $7 \times 6 = \boxed{}$

2 $2 \times 6 = \boxed{}$

3 $5 \times 6 = \boxed{}$

4 $10 \times 6 = \boxed{}$

5 $4 \times 6 = \boxed{}$

6 $12 \times 6 = \boxed{}$

7 $0 \times 6 = \boxed{}$

8 $8 \times 6 = \boxed{}$

9 $11 \times 6 = \boxed{}$

10 $6 \times 6 = \boxed{}$

11 $9 \times 6 = \boxed{}$

12 $3 \times 6 = \boxed{}$

13 $24 \div 6 = \boxed{}$

14 $6 \div 6 = \boxed{}$

15 $42 \div 6 = \boxed{}$

16 $66 \div 6 = \boxed{}$

17 $48 \div 6 = \boxed{}$

18 $12 \div 6 = \boxed{}$

19 $60 \div 6 = \boxed{}$

20 $36 \div 6 = \boxed{}$

21 $18 \div 6 = \boxed{}$

22 $72 \div 6 = \boxed{}$

23 $30 \div 6 = \boxed{}$

24 $54 \div 6 = \boxed{}$

25 $\boxed{} \times 6 = 60$

26 $\boxed{} \times 6 = 36$

27 $\boxed{} \times 6 = 18$

28 $\boxed{} \times 6 = 54$

29 $\boxed{} \times 6 = 30$

30 $\boxed{} \times 6 = 12$

31 $\boxed{} \times 6 = 48$

32 $\boxed{} \times 6 = 66$

33 $\boxed{} \times 6 = 72$

34 $\boxed{} \times 6 = 0$

35 $\boxed{} \times 6 = 42$

36 $\boxed{} \times 6 = 24$

37 $\boxed{} \div 6 = 4$

38 $\boxed{} \div 6 = 9$

39 $\boxed{} \div 6 = 2$

40 $\boxed{} \div 6 = 6$

41 $\boxed{} \div 6 = 11$

42 $\boxed{} \div 6 = 3$

43 $\boxed{} \div 6 = 7$

44 $\boxed{} \div 6 = 10$

45 $\boxed{} \div 6 = 5$

46 $\boxed{} \div 6 = 1$

47 $\boxed{} \div 6 = 12$

48 $\boxed{} \div 6 = 8$

Colour in the diagrams to show each pair of equivalent fractions.
Write the missing fraction.

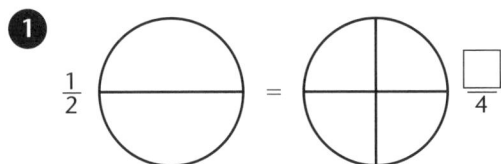

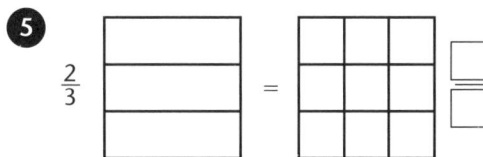

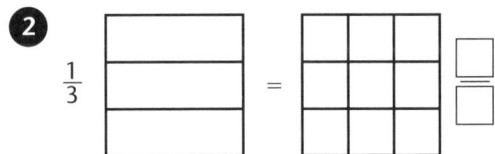

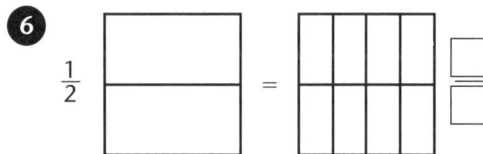

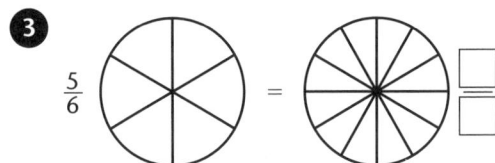

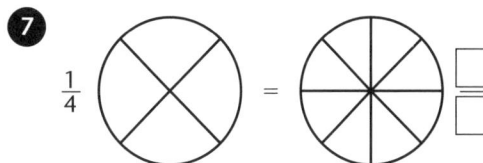

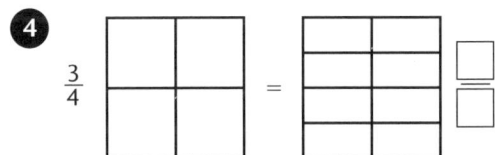

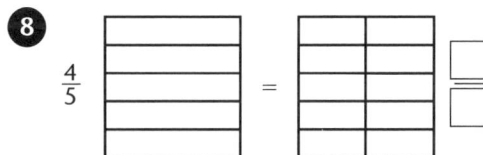

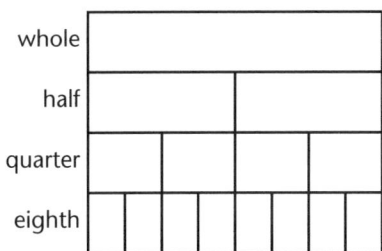

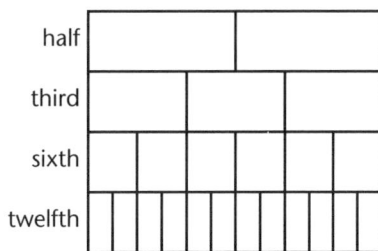

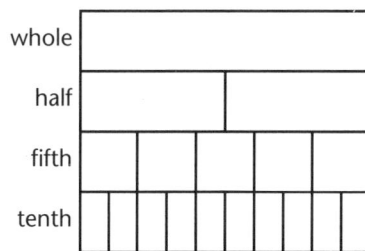

1 $\frac{1}{2}$ = $\frac{\square}{4}$

5 $\frac{2}{3}$ = $\frac{\square}{\square}$

2 $\frac{1}{3}$ = $\frac{\square}{\square}$

6 $\frac{1}{2}$ = $\frac{\square}{\square}$

3 $\frac{5}{6}$ = $\frac{\square}{\square}$

7 $\frac{1}{4}$ = $\frac{\square}{\square}$

4 $\frac{3}{4}$ = $\frac{\square}{\square}$

8 $\frac{4}{5}$ = $\frac{\square}{\square}$

whole	
half	
quarter	
eighth	

half	
third	
sixth	
twelfth	

whole	
half	
fifth	
tenth	

Use the fraction charts to complete the equivalent fractions.

9 $\frac{1}{6} = \frac{\square}{12}$

11 $\frac{1}{4} = \frac{\square}{12}$

13 $\frac{1}{2} = \frac{\square}{10}$

15 $\frac{2}{3} = \frac{\square}{9}$

10 $\frac{2}{5} = \frac{\square}{10}$

12 $\frac{2}{3} = \frac{\square}{6}$

14 $\frac{3}{4} = \frac{\square}{8}$

16 $\frac{4}{5} = \frac{\square}{10}$

For each of the times:

a) draw the hands on the clock face

b) write the time in 12-hour clock time.

1. 17 minutes past 4 (afternoon)
2. 17 minutes to 4 (night)
3. 1 minute past 10 (night)
4. 25 minutes past 10 (morning)
5. 8 minutes to 2 (afternoon)
6. 22 minutes to 1 (night)

For each of the times:

a) draw the hands on the clock face

b) write the time in 24-hour clock time.

7. 9 minutes past 6 (morning)
8. 14 minutes past 12 (lunchtime)
9. 3 minutes to 3 (night)
10. 27 minutes to 7 (evening)
11. 21 minutes past 8 (morning)
12. 19 minutes to 12 (night)

Work out

1

4:17 pm

4

7

10

2

5

8

11

3

6

9

12

Complete the table.

No.	Time in Words	12-Hour Clock	24-Hour Clock
1	25 minutes to 10	9:35 am	
2		10:05 pm	
3		4: 52 am	
4		1:10 pm	
5		11:41 am	
6		2:23 pm	
7			05:08
8			20:57
9			01:34
10			12:12
11			15:46
12			07:29

For each of the above times work out how many minutes there are to the next hour.

1 ....25.........   **5** ....   **9** ....

2 ....   **6** ....   **10** ....

3 ....   **7** ....   **11** ....

4 ....   **8** ....   **12** ....

The shapes are:

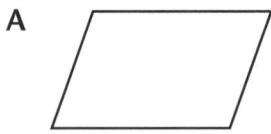

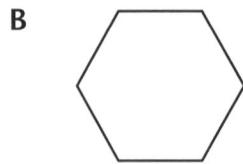

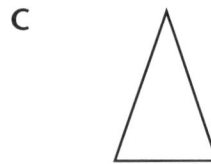

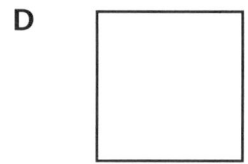

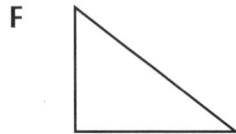

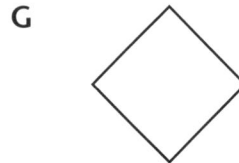

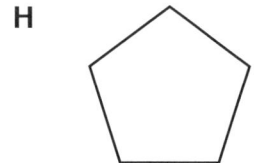

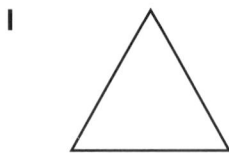

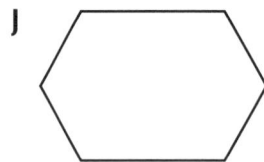

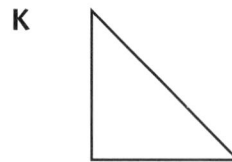

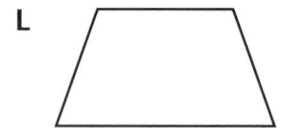

A   B   C   D

E   F   G   H

I   J   K   L

Write down the letter to identify the shape.

1 Which of the shapes are triangles?   ....

2 Which of the triangles are isosceles?   ....

3 Which of the shapes are quadrilaterals?   ....

4 Which of the quadrilaterals have equal opposite sides?   ....

5 Which of the shapes have more than 4 sides?   ....

6 Which of the shapes are regular?   ....

7 Which of the shapes are irregular?   ....

8 Which of the shapes have 2 or more pairs of parallel lines?   ....

9 Which of the shapes have 2 or more right angles?   ....

10 Which of the shapes have 2 or more obtuse angles?   ....

11 Which of the shapes have 2 or more acute angles?   ....

12 Which of the shapes are not symmetrical?   ....

Write the missing number in the box.

1 $5 \times 7 =$ ☐

2 $8 \times 7 =$ ☐

3 $1 \times 7 =$ ☐

4 $12 \times 7 =$ ☐

5 $7 \times 7 =$ ☐

6 $3 \times 7 =$ ☐

7 $10 \times 7 =$ ☐

8 $4 \times 7 =$ ☐

9 $2 \times 7 =$ ☐

10 $11 \times 7 =$ ☐

11 $6 \times 7 =$ ☐

12 $9 \times 7 =$ ☐

13 $28 \div 7 =$ ☐

14 $70 \div 7 =$ ☐

15 $14 \div 7 =$ ☐

16 $49 \div 7 =$ ☐

17 $63 \div 7 =$ ☐

18 $42 \div 7 =$ ☐

19 $77 \div 7 =$ ☐

20 $0 \div 7 =$ ☐

21 $84 \div 7 =$ ☐

22 $21 \div 7 =$ ☐

23 $56 \div 7 =$ ☐

24 $35 \div 7 =$ ☐

25   ☐ $\times 7 = 42$

26   ☐ $\times 7 = 77$

27   ☐ $\times 7 = 21$

28   ☐ $\times 7 = 63$

29   ☐ $\times 7 = 14$

30   ☐ $\times 7 = 56$

31   ☐ $\times 7 = 35$

32   ☐ $\times 7 = 84$

33   ☐ $\times 7 = 28$

34   ☐ $\times 7 = 70$

35   ☐ $\times 7 = 7$

36   ☐ $\times 7 = 49$

37   ☐ $\div 7 = 7$

38   ☐ $\div 7 = 4$

39   ☐ $\div 7 = 0$

40   ☐ $\div 7 = 10$

41   ☐ $\div 7 = 6$

42   ☐ $\div 7 = 11$

43   ☐ $\div 7 = 8$

44   ☐ $\div 7 = 3$

45   ☐ $\div 7 = 5$

46   ☐ $\div 7 = 2$

47   ☐ $\div 7 = 9$

48   ☐ $\div 7 = 12$

Sheet 12   WRITTEN METHOD ×/÷ 1

Examples	4 8 3	270 ÷ 6
	× 7	4 5
	3 3 8 1	6)2 7³0
	5 2	

Work out

1   2 7 4
  ×   8

4   7 4 8
  ×   4

7   3 7 6
  ×   6

2   8 0 6
  ×   3

5   3 6 5
  ×   7

8   1 5 8
  ×   8

3   5 2 9
  ×   6

6   6 8 7
  ×   5

9   2 4 9
  ×   7

Work out

10 $102 ÷ 6 = $ ☐

6)1 0 2

13 $156 ÷ 2 = $ ☐

2)1 5 6

16 $210 ÷ 6 = $ ☐

6)2 1 0

11 $140 ÷ 4 = $ ☐

4)1 4 0

14 $182 ÷ 7 = $ ☐

7)1 8 2

17 $136 ÷ 8 = $ ☐

8)1 3 6

12 $192 ÷ 8 = $ ☐

8)1 9 2

15 $145 ÷ 5 = $ ☐

5)1 4 5

18 $237 ÷ 3 = $ ☐

3)2 3 7

Write the decimal fraction shown by each arrow in the box.

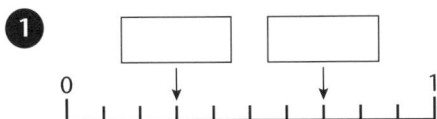

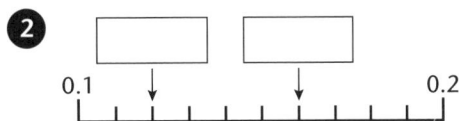

1

2

Write as a decimal.

3 $\frac{2}{10}$ ....

4 $\frac{58}{100}$ ....

5 $\frac{1}{2}$ ....

6 $\frac{1}{100}$ ....

7 $\frac{74}{100}$ ....

8 $\frac{1}{4}$ ....

9 $\frac{20}{100}$ ....

10 $\frac{9}{10}$ ....

11 $\frac{3}{4}$ ....

12 $\frac{6}{100}$ ....

13 $\frac{5}{10}$ ....

14 $\frac{32}{100}$ ....

Write as fractions.

15 0·95 ....

16 0·04 ....

17 0·37 ....

18 0·5 ....

19 0·82 ....

20 0·1 ....

21 0·75 ....

22 0·09 ....

23 0·25 ....

24 0·53 ....

25 0·6 ....

26 0·41 ....

Give the value of the underlined decimal.

27 0·3<u>4</u> ....

28 0·0<u>2</u> ....

29 0·<u>5</u>7 ....

30 0·<u>8</u> ....

31 0·<u>6</u>2 ....

32 0·9<u>8</u> ....

33 0·0<u>5</u> ....

34 0·2<u>1</u> ....

35 0·8<u>3</u> ....

36 0·<u>4</u> ....

37 0·<u>7</u>6 ....

38 0·1<u>9</u> ....

Write the missing number in the box.

1 40 mm = ▢ cm

2 115 mm = ▢ cm

3 3 mm = ▢ cm

4 79 mm = ▢ cm

5 1010 cm = ▢ m

6 540 cm = ▢ m

7 200 cm = ▢ m

8 70 cm = ▢ m

9 3600 m = ▢ km

10 200 m = ▢ km

11 5800 m = ▢ km

12 9000 m = ▢ km

13 1300 g = ▢ kg

14 900 g = ▢ kg

15 4700 g = ▢ kg

16 8000 g = ▢ kg

17 2500 ml = ▢ litres

18 400 ml = ▢ litres

19 6000 ml = ▢ litres

20 3800 ml = ▢ litres

21 3·2 cm = ▢ mm

22 0·6 cm = ▢ mm

23 12·0 cm = ▢ mm

24 5·0 cm = ▢ mm

25 20·0 m = ▢ cm

26 0·2 m = ▢ cm

27 3·0 m = ▢ cm

28 8·5 m = ▢ cm

29 4·0 km = ▢ m

30 1·3 km = ▢ m

31 0·7 km = ▢ m

32 6·4 km = ▢ m

33 2·6 kg = ▢ g

34 9·8 kg = ▢ g

35 0·5 kg = ▢ g

36 3·0 kg = ▢ g

37 5·2 litres = ▢ ml

38 1·9 litres = ▢ ml

39 7·0 litres = ▢ ml

40 0·1 litres = ▢ ml

1 These are the ages of the children in the Junior Section of a Tennis Club.

Age	Number of children
7	6
8	9
9	12
10	14
11	17
12	15

Use the grid to draw a vertical bar chart labelled in twos to show the information.

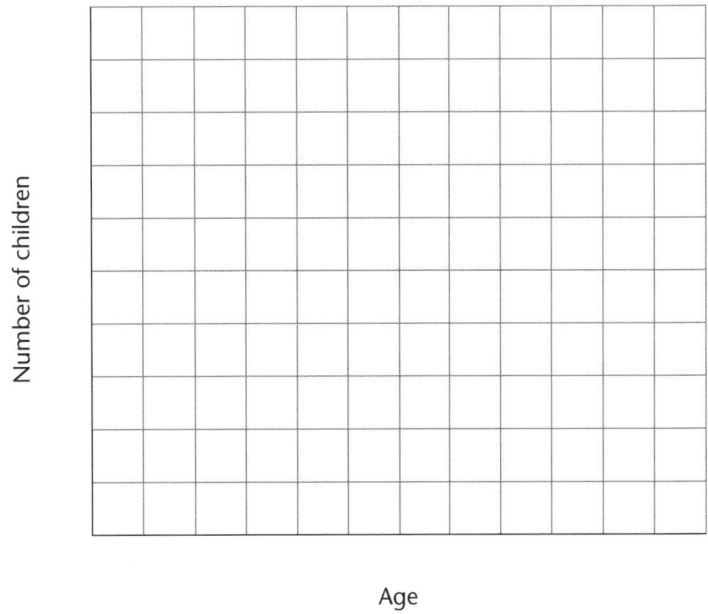

Number of children

Age

2 This table shows the number of students studying different languages at a Language School.

Language	Number of students
Arabic	60
Chinese	95
French	35
German	85
Hindi	40
Spanish	70

Use the grid to draw a horizontal bar chart labelled in tens to show the information. Remember to label the axes.

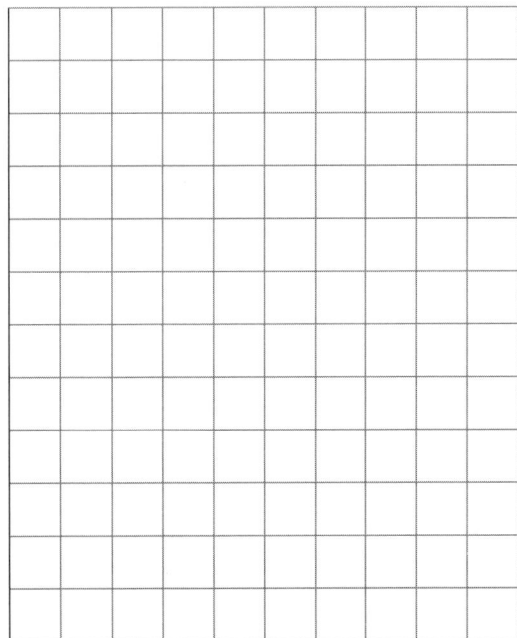

Write the missing number in the box.

1 $4 \times 9 = \boxed{}$

2 $11 \times 9 = \boxed{}$

3 $2 \times 9 = \boxed{}$

4 $9 \times 9 = \boxed{}$

5 $6 \times 9 = \boxed{}$

6 $0 \times 9 = \boxed{}$

7 $10 \times 9 = \boxed{}$

8 $8 \times 9 = \boxed{}$

9 $3 \times 9 = \boxed{}$

10 $7 \times 9 = \boxed{}$

11 $5 \times 9 = \boxed{}$

12 $12 \times 9 = \boxed{}$

13 $90 \div 9 = \boxed{}$

14 $27 \div 9 = \boxed{}$

15 $54 \div 9 = \boxed{}$

16 $72 \div 9 = \boxed{}$

17 $9 \div 9 = \boxed{}$

18 $45 \div 9 = \boxed{}$

19 $108 \div 9 = \boxed{}$

20 $63 \div 9 = \boxed{}$

21 $36 \div 9 = \boxed{}$

22 $18 \div 9 = \boxed{}$

23 $81 \div 9 = \boxed{}$

24 $99 \div 9 = \boxed{}$

25 $\boxed{} \times 9 = 63$

26 $\boxed{} \times 9 = 45$

27 $\boxed{} \times 9 = 0$

28 $\boxed{} \times 9 = 108$

29 $\boxed{} \times 9 = 81$

30 $\boxed{} \times 9 = 36$

31 $\boxed{} \times 9 = 90$

32 $\boxed{} \times 9 = 18$

33 $\boxed{} \times 9 = 54$

34 $\boxed{} \times 9 = 27$

35 $\boxed{} \times 9 = 99$

36 $\boxed{} \times 9 = 72$

37 $\boxed{} \div 9 = 10$

38 $\boxed{} \div 9 = 3$

39 $\boxed{} \div 9 = 8$

40 $\boxed{} \div 9 = 5$

41 $\boxed{} \div 9 = 11$

42 $\boxed{} \div 9 = 6$

43 $\boxed{} \div 9 = 1$

44 $\boxed{} \div 9 = 9$

45 $\boxed{} \div 9 = 2$

46 $\boxed{} \div 9 = 7$

47 $\boxed{} \div 9 = 4$

48 $\boxed{} \div 9 = 12$

Work out

1 90×3 ....

2 700×6 ....

3 80×20 ....

4 60×8 ....

5 5×70 ....

6 8×400 ....

7 30×60 ....

8 4×90 ....

9 6×500 ....

10 90×80 ....

11 $150 \div 5$ ....

12 $6300 \div 7$ ....

13 $3600 \div 6$ ....

14 $180 \div 2$ ....

15 $2700 \div 9$ ....

16 $2400 \div 30$ ....

17 $490 \div 70$ ....

18 $4000 \div 80$ ....

19 $240 \div 40$ ....

20 $8100 \div 90$ ....

Write the answer in the box.

21 [   ] $\times 2 = 1200$

22 [   ] $\times 7 = 560$

23 [   ] $\times 30 = 150$

24 [   ] $\times 6 = 540$

25 [   ] $\times 9 = 6300$

26 [   ] $\times 50 = 450$

27 [   ] $\times 8 = 6400$

28 [   ] $\times 4 = 200$

29 [   ] $\times 90 = 540$

30 [   ] $\times 7 = 280$

31 [   ] $\div 3 = 70$

32 [   ] $\div 6 = 800$

33 [   ] $\div 8 = 400$

34 [   ] $\div 4 = 90$

35 [   ] $\div 2 = 700$

36 [   ] $\div 70 = 6$

37 [   ] $\div 50 = 90$

38 [   ] $\div 80 = 70$

39 [   ] $\div 60 = 5$

40 [   ] $\div 90 = 80$

Fill in the boxes.

1 Sophie is 12. Her grandmother is seven times older.

Sophie's grandmother is ☐ .

2 One tenth of 800 is ☐ .

3 There are nine stacks of 6 chairs. There are ☐ chairs.

4 ☐ multiplied by 7 gives an answer of 280.

5 Four hours is ☐ minutes.

6 ☐ multiplied by itself is 81.

7 Twenty £50 notes is £☐ .

8 Eighty tea bags weigh 240 g. One tea bag weighs ☐ g.

9 Eleven footballers are needed for one team.

☐ footballers are needed for twelve teams.

10 There are 280 children in a school. One quarter are in Year 3.
Year 3 has ☐ children.

11 Each packet holds eight apples. There are ☐ apples in nine packets.

12 Each box holds twelve pencils. There are 60 pencils in ☐ boxes.

13 Six weeks is ☐ days.

14 121 is ☐ multiplied by ☐ .

15 One can weighs 400 g. Eight cans weigh ☐ g.

16 One quarter of a 2 litre can of paint is used. ☐ ml is left.

1 Measure the length and width of the rectangle to the nearest millimetre.
Fill in the missing lengths to work out the perimeter.

Length .... cm × 2 = ... cm

Width .... cm × 2 = ... cm

Perimeter = ... cm

For each of these shapes find the area and the perimeter.

2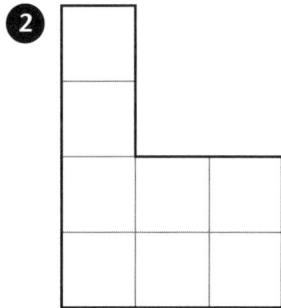

3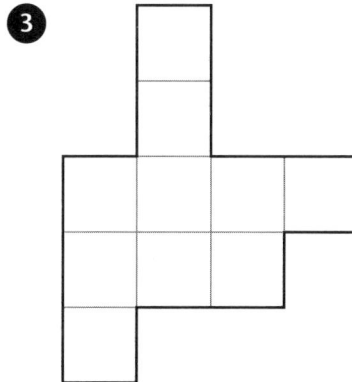

4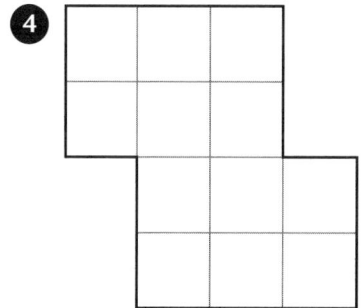

Area   .... cm²

Perimeter .... cm

Area   .... cm²

Perimeter .... cm

Area   .... cm²

Perimeter .... cm

5 Draw a rectangle with a perimeter of 20 cm. Work out the area.

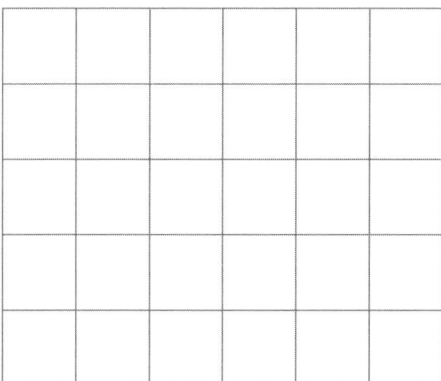

Area .... cm²

6 Draw a rectangle with an area of 20 cm². Work out the perimeter.

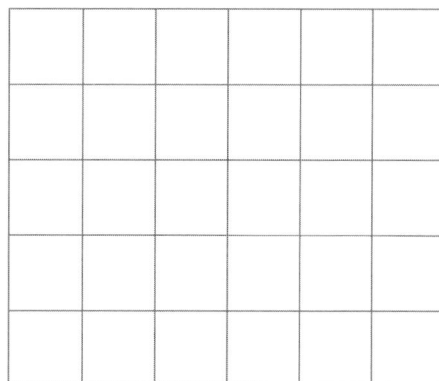

Perimeter .... cm

Write the angles in each group in order, smallest first.

1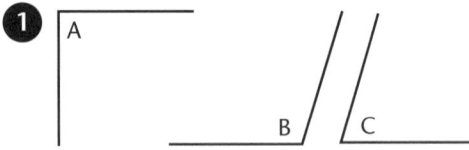

Order ....

2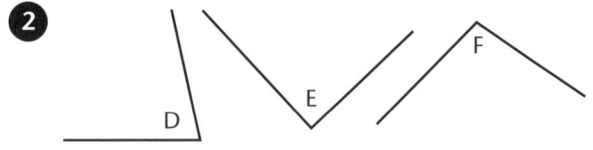

Order ....

3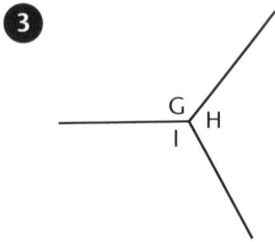

Order ....

4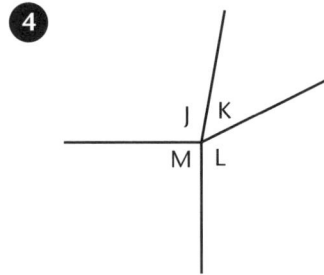

Order ....

5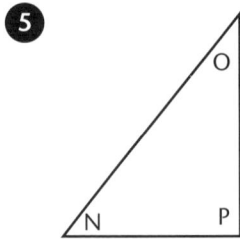

Order ....

6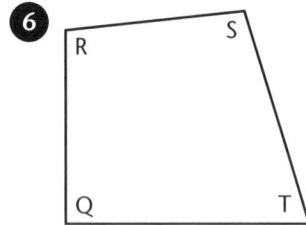

Order ....

7 Write acute, obtuse or right angle for each of the above angles.

A	....	H	....	O	....
B	....	I	....	P	....
C	....	J	....	Q	....
D	....	K	....	R	....
E	....	L	....	S	....
F	....	M	....	T	....
G	....	N	....		

Write down the number you reach if you count on:

1 six steps of 2 from 12 ....   **7** six steps of 9 from 18 ....

2 five steps of 5 from 45 ....   **8** seven steps of 6 from 12 ....

3 seven steps of 8 from 16 ....   **9** nine steps of 5 from 70 ....

4 nine steps of 4 from 20 ....   **10** eight steps of 4 from 100 ....

5 four steps of 3 from 15 ....   **11** seven steps of 2 from 28 ....

6 eight steps of 7 from 0 ....   **12** nine steps of 3 from 18 ....

Write down the number you reach if you count on:

13 70 from 1240 ....   **18** 90 from 2364 ....

14 500 from 3820 ....   **19** 600 from 1438 ....

15 3000 from 6190 ....   **20** 5000 from 607 ....

16 four 50s from 8500 ....   **21** seven 50s from 5905 ....

17 six 25s from 1750 ....   **22** eight 25s from 7550 ....

Write down the number you reach.

23 Count back 3 from 0. ....   **28** Count on 7 from −1. ....

24 Count on 4 from −3. ....   **29** Count back 9 from 5. ....

25 Count back 5 from 3. ....   **30** Count on 6 from −6. ....

26 Count on 8 from −4. ....   **31** Count back 3 from 2. ....

27 Count back 6 from 1. ....   **32** Count on 9 from −7. ....

To round to the nearest 10 look at the units column.
To round to the nearest 100 look at the tens column.
To round to the nearest 1000 look at the hundreds column.
If the number is less than 5, round down.
If the number is 5 or greater than 5, round up.

Round these numbers to the nearest

(10)   (100)   (1000)

1 1723 ....   **11** 3472 ....   **21** 1329 ....

2 2438 ....   **12** 1645 ....   **22** 4542 ....

3 5395 ....   **13** 7318 ....   **23** 3675 ....

4 8671 ....   **14** 4251 ....   **24** 5138 ....

5 3827 ....   **15** 6936 ....   **25** 2881 ....

6 4069 ....   **16** 2164 ....   **26** 6254 ....

7 6504 ....   **17** 8583 ....   **27** 8906 ....

8 2182 ....   **18** 6727 ....   **28** 7590 ....

9 7946 ....   **19** 3859 ....   **29** 2417 ....

10 9215 ....   **20** 7992 ....   **30** 6763 ....

Approximate by rounding to the nearest 10.

31 476 + 283 ⟶ ☐ + ☐ = ☐

32 917 − 365 ⟶ ☐ − ☐ = ☐

33 762 + 539 ⟶ ☐ + ☐ = ☐

34 1528 − 671 ⟶ ☐ − ☐ = ☐

35 74 × 3 ⟶ ☐ × 3 = ☐

36 59 × 8 ⟶ ☐ × 8 = ☐

Write the missing number in the box.

1 $50 + 80 =$ ☐

2 $30 + 90 =$ ☐

3 $90 + 80 =$ ☐

4 $40 +$ ☐ $= 110$

5 $90 +$ ☐ $= 180$

6 $80 +$ ☐ $= 140$

7 $800 + 800 =$ ☐

8 $700 + 500 =$ ☐

9 $300 + 800 =$ ☐

10 $900 +$ ☐ $= 1500$

11 $600 +$ ☐ $= 1300$

12 $500 +$ ☐ $= 1400$

13 $100 - 28 =$ ☐

14 $100 - 54 =$ ☐

15 $100 - 7 =$ ☐

16 $100 -$ ☐ $= 61$

17 $100 -$ ☐ $= 15$

18 $100 -$ ☐ $= 76$

19 $190 - 50 =$ ☐

20 $120 - 60 =$ ☐

21 $150 - 70 =$ ☐

22 $200 -$ ☐ $= 130$

23 $140 -$ ☐ $= 70$

24 $130 -$ ☐ $= 90$

25 $1800 - 1300 =$ ☐

26 $1100 - 500 =$ ☐

27 $2000 - 800 =$ ☐

28 $1600 -$ ☐ $= 700$

29 $1700 -$ ☐ $= 300$

30 $1200 -$ ☐ $= 400$

31 $43 +$ ☐ $= 100$

32 $92 +$ ☐ $= 100$

33 $35 +$ ☐ $= 100$

34 ☐ $+ 84 = 100$

35 ☐ $+ 29 = 100$

36 ☐ $+ 51 = 100$

	Examples	4 7 5 9 + 3 3 8 6	8 10 13 1 9̶ X̶ 4̶ 7 − 2 8 5 9
		8 1 4 5 1 1 1	6 2 8 8

Work out

1   5 6 9 5
      + 1 8 6 7
      _____

2   2 9 4 7
      + 2 2 6 8
      _____

3   4 3 8 6
      + 3 6 5 9
      _____

4   8 1 4 8
      − 5 7 9 5
      _____

5   4 7 5 0
      − 2 3 8 2
      _____

6   7 2 9 3
      − 1 6 2 4
      _____

7   3 4 7 8
      + 1 8 7 4
      _____

8   5 7 5 9
      + 3 4 9 7
      _____

9   6 8 6 3
      + 2 1 4 8
      _____

10 9 0 6 2
      − 4 5 3 5
      _____

11 5 4 3 8
      − 1 7 8 4
      _____

12 3 5 7 0
      − 2 1 9 7
      _____

13 2 5 8 4
      + 1 5 6 9
      _____

14 3 9 7 6
      + 2 5 3 7
      _____

15 4 2 9 8
      + 2 7 0 9
      _____

16 6 9 2 5
      − 3 7 9 6
      _____

17 8 3 4 1
      − 2 5 0 8
      _____

18 9 5 1 7
      − 4 9 3 2
      _____

Write the missing number in the box.

1 $7 \times 5 = \boxed{}$

2 $1 \times 4 = \boxed{}$

3 $6 \times 10 = \boxed{}$

4 $\boxed{} \times 5 = 55$

5 $\boxed{} \times 4 = 36$

6 $\boxed{} \times 10 = 100$

7 $\boxed{} \div 5 = 8$

8 $\boxed{} \div 4 = 12$

9 $\boxed{} \div 10 = 5$

10 $8 \times 2 = \boxed{}$

11 $4 \times 8 = \boxed{}$

12 $11 \times 3 = \boxed{}$

13 $\boxed{} \times 2 = 24$

14 $\boxed{} \times 8 = 56$

15 $\boxed{} \times 3 = 0$

16 $\boxed{} \div 2 = 7$

17 $\boxed{} \div 8 = 9$

18 $\boxed{} \div 3 = 6$

19 $4 \times 6 = \boxed{}$

20 $9 \times 6 = \boxed{}$

21 $2 \times 6 = \boxed{}$

22 $\boxed{} \times 6 = 42$

23 $\boxed{} \times 6 = 18$

24 $\boxed{} \times 6 = 72$

25 $\boxed{} \div 6 = 5$

26 $\boxed{} \div 6 = 8$

27 $\boxed{} \div 6 = 6$

28 $6 \times 7 = \boxed{}$

29 $3 \times 7 = \boxed{}$

30 $8 \times 7 = \boxed{}$

31 $\boxed{} \times 7 = 35$

32 $\boxed{} \times 7 = 49$

33 $\boxed{} \times 7 = 77$

34 $\boxed{} \div 7 = 4$

35 $\boxed{} \div 7 = 12$

36 $\boxed{} \div 7 = 9$

37 $5 \times 9 = \boxed{}$

38 $7 \times 9 = \boxed{}$

39 $9 \times 9 = \boxed{}$

40 $\boxed{} \times 9 = 36$

41 $\boxed{} \times 9 = 54$

42 $\boxed{} \times 9 = 108$

43 $\boxed{} \div 9 = 10$

44 $\boxed{} \div 9 = 3$

45 $\boxed{} \div 9 = 8$

Write the missing number in the box.

1 $5 \times 11 = \boxed{}$

2 $10 \times 11 = \boxed{}$

3 $3 \times 11 = \boxed{}$

4 $8 \times 11 = \boxed{}$

5 $1 \times 11 = \boxed{}$

6 $9 \times 11 = \boxed{}$

7 $4 \times 11 = \boxed{}$

8 $12 \times 11 = \boxed{}$

9 $7 \times 11 = \boxed{}$

10 $2 \times 11 = \boxed{}$

11 $11 \times 11 = \boxed{}$

12 $6 \times 11 = \boxed{}$

13 $99 \div 11 = \boxed{}$

14 $11 \div 11 = \boxed{}$

15 $66 \div 11 = \boxed{}$

16 $121 \div 11 = \boxed{}$

17 $22 \div 11 = \boxed{}$

18 $55 \div 11 = \boxed{}$

19 $110 \div 11 = \boxed{}$

20 $77 \div 11 = \boxed{}$

21 $33 \div 11 = \boxed{}$

22 $88 \div 11 = \boxed{}$

23 $132 \div 11 = \boxed{}$

24 $44 \div 11 = \boxed{}$

25 $\boxed{} \times 11 = 22$

26 $\boxed{} \times 11 = 77$

27 $\boxed{} \times 11 = 132$

28 $\boxed{} \times 11 = 44$

29 $\boxed{} \times 11 = 121$

30 $\boxed{} \times 11 = 66$

31 $\boxed{} \times 11 = 33$

32 $\boxed{} \times 11 = 88$

33 $\boxed{} \times 11 = 0$

34 $\boxed{} \times 11 = 110$

35 $\boxed{} \times 11 = 55$

36 $\boxed{} \times 11 = 99$

37 $\boxed{} \div 11 = 3$

38 $\boxed{} \div 11 = 10$

39 $\boxed{} \div 11 = 8$

40 $\boxed{} \div 11 = 6$

41 $\boxed{} \div 11 = 7$

42 $\boxed{} \div 11 = 2$

43 $\boxed{} \div 11 = 5$

44 $\boxed{} \div 11 = 12$

45 $\boxed{} \div 11 = 4$

46 $\boxed{} \div 11 = 11$

47 $\boxed{} \div 11 = 1$

48 $\boxed{} \div 11 = 9$

Examples	$\begin{array}{r} 6\ 2\ 9 \\ \times\ \ \ \ \ 9 \\ \hline 5\ 6\ 6\ 1 \\ \small 2\ 8 \end{array}$	$\begin{array}{r} 2\ 6 \\ 7\overline{)1\ 8^4 2} \end{array}$

Work out

1
$$\begin{array}{r} 5\ 4\ 8 \\ \times\ \ \ \ \ 7 \\ \hline \end{array}$$

2
$$\begin{array}{r} 7\ 9\ 4 \\ \times\ \ \ \ \ 6 \\ \hline \end{array}$$

3
$$\begin{array}{r} 6\ 5\ 7 \\ \times\ \ \ \ \ 2 \\ \hline \end{array}$$

4
$$\begin{array}{r} 3\ 7\ 5 \\ \times\ \ \ \ \ 9 \\ \hline \end{array}$$

5
$$\begin{array}{r} 9\ 7\ 4 \\ \times\ \ \ \ \ 5 \\ \hline \end{array}$$

6
$$\begin{array}{r} 5\ 2\ 9 \\ \times\ \ \ \ \ 8 \\ \hline \end{array}$$

7
$$\begin{array}{r} 7\ 9\ 6 \\ \times\ \ \ \ \ 7 \\ \hline \end{array}$$

8
$$\begin{array}{r} 4\ 6\ 5 \\ \times\ \ \ \ \ 4 \\ \hline \end{array}$$

9
$$\begin{array}{r} 2\ 8\ 7 \\ \times\ \ \ \ \ 6 \\ \hline \end{array}$$

10
$$\begin{array}{r} 8\ 4\ 6 \\ \times\ \ \ \ \ 9 \\ \hline \end{array}$$

11
$$\begin{array}{r} 9\ 7\ 5 \\ \times\ \ \ \ \ 3 \\ \hline \end{array}$$

12
$$\begin{array}{r} 4\ 6\ 7 \\ \times\ \ \ \ \ 8 \\ \hline \end{array}$$

13 $9\overline{)2\ 2\ 5}$

14 $7\overline{)1\ 1\ 9}$

15 $5\overline{)1\ 8\ 0}$

16 $8\overline{)1\ 5\ 2}$

17 $6\overline{)2\ 1\ 6}$

18 $4\overline{)2\ 3\ 2}$

19 $9\overline{)4\ 2\ 3}$

20 $2\overline{)1\ 3\ 8}$

21 $7\overline{)2\ 6\ 6}$

22 $3\overline{)1\ 9\ 5}$

23 $8\overline{)2\ 8\ 8}$

24 $6\overline{)2\ 9\ 4}$

Change to pounds.

1 73p ....£0·73.......

2 126p ....

3 41p ....

4 590p ....

5 1805p ....

6 8p ....

Change to centimetres.

7 62 mm ....

8 9 mm ....

9 104 mm ....

10 7 mm ....

11 293 mm ....

12 15 mm ....

Change to metres.

13 338 cm ....

14 970 cm ....

15 6 cm ....

16 2451 cm ....

17 19 cm ....

18 702 cm ....

Write the measurement shown by each arrow.

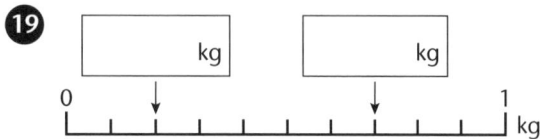

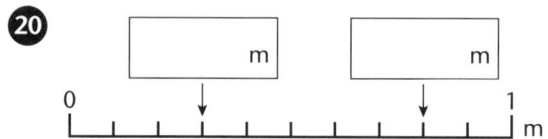

19

| kg | | kg |

0 .... 1 kg

20

| m | | m |

0 .... 1 m

Write the value of the underlined figure.

21 £4·2<u>8</u>   ......8p......

22 £0·<u>5</u>3 ....

23 £6·<u>8</u>0 ....

24 13·0<u>9</u> m ....

25 1·<u>6</u>5 m ....

26 4<u>7</u>·17 m ....

27 £0·9<u>4</u> ....

28 £<u>5</u>2·71 ....

29 £8·3<u>6</u> ....

30 <u>5</u>·87 kg ....

31 0·4<u>8</u> kg ....

32 13·0<u>2</u> kg ....

33 £9·<u>5</u>7 ....

34 £4·2<u>3</u> ....

35 £3<u>1</u>·99 ....

36 7·<u>6</u>1 km ....

37 <u>2</u>6·05 km ....

38 3·8<u>4</u> km ....

Give the next four terms in each sequence.

39 £0·95, £0·96, £0·97, £0·98   ....

40 0·02 m, 0·04 m, 0·06 m, 0·08 m   ....

Write the missing number in the box.

1 2·0 cm = [   ] mm

2 0·9 cm = [   ] mm

3 7·5 cm = [   ] mm

4 3·8 cm = [   ] mm

5 0·5 m = [   ] cm

6 5 m = [   ] cm

7 0·37 m = [   ] cm

8 1·55 m = [   ] cm

9 0·6 km = [   ] m

10 6 km = [   ] m

11 2·1 km = [   ] m

12 0·42 km = [   ] m

13 1·2 kg = [   ] g

14 3·96 kg = [   ] g

15 0·01 kg = [   ] g

16 5·8 kg = [   ] g

17 0·7 litres = [   ] ml

18 2·59 litres = [   ] ml

19 4 litres = [   ] ml

20 0·25 litres = [   ] ml

21 51 mm = [   ] cm

22 10 mm = [   ] cm

23 6 mm = [   ] cm

24 93 mm = [   ] cm

25 345 cm = [   ] m

26 80 cm = [   ] m

27 820 cm = [   ] m

28 403 cm = [   ] m

29 1780 m = [   ] km

30 7200 m = [   ] km

31 20 m = [   ] km

32 5460 m = [   ] km

33 500 g = [   ] kg

34 2340 g = [   ] kg

35 6050 g = [   ] kg

36 900 g = [   ] kg

37 3220 ml = [   ] litres

38 800 ml = [   ] litres

39 1600 ml = [   ] litres

40 70 ml = [   ] litres

1 Use these names to label each shape.

equilateral triangle   quadrilateral   square
isosceles triangle   rhombus   trapezium

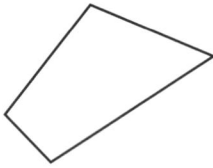

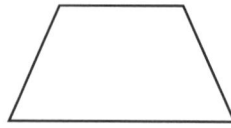

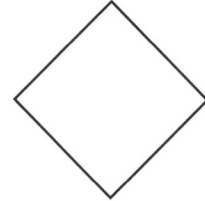

A ....   B ....   C ....

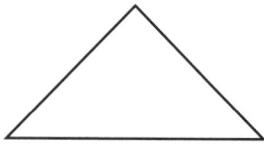

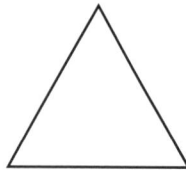

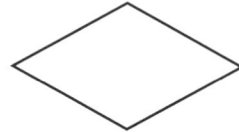

D ....   E ....   F ....

....

2 Draw the shape in each grid with its corners on the dots.

scalene triangle   rectangle   quadrilateral   right-angled triangle

parallelogram   isosceles triangle   rhombus   trapezium

The position of a point on a grid is given by its x and y co-ordinates

The x co-ordinate always comes first.

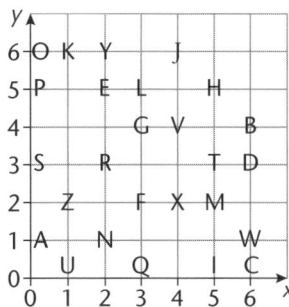

Use the above grid.
Which letter?

Give the co-ordinates.

1 (6, 4) ....   **5** (0, 3) ....   **9** G ....   **13** J ....

2 (1, 6) ....   **6** (5, 5) ....   **10** I ....   **14** W ....

3 (3, 0) ....   **7** (2, 1) ....   **11** Z ....   **15** R ....

4 (4, 2) ....   **8** (6, 0) ....   **12** P ....   **16** F ....

Use the above grid. Write these names in co-ordinates.

17 VINOD ....

18 LUCY ....

19 DAVIE ....

20 GEMMA ....

Use the above grid. Start at the co-ordinate given. Follow the directions.
Write down the letter you find.

21 (6, 2)   Left 4 Up 1 ....   **25** (1, 3)   Right 4 Up 2 ....

22 (3, 0)   Right 2 Up 3 ....   **26** (4, 4)   Right 2 Down 3 ....

23 (5, 4)   Left 2 Down 2 ....   **27** (4, 1)   Left 3 Up 5 ....

24 (0, 5)   Right 3 Down 5 ....   **28** (6, 6)   Left 5 Down 4 ....

Write the missing number in the box.

1 2 × 12 = ☐

2 7 × 12 = ☐

3 11 × 12 = ☐

4 4 × 12 = ☐

5 8 × 12 = ☐

6 3 × 12 = ☐

7 10 × 12 = ☐

8 6 × 12 = ☐

9 0 × 12 = ☐

10 9 × 12 = ☐

11 5 × 12 = ☐

12 12 × 12 = ☐

13 60 ÷ 12 = ☐

14 96 ÷ 12 = ☐

15 36 ÷ 12 = ☐

16 120 ÷ 12 = ☐

17 12 ÷ 12 = ☐

18 144 ÷ 12 = ☐

19 48 ÷ 12 = ☐

20 108 ÷ 12 = ☐

21 72 ÷ 12 = ☐

22 24 ÷ 12 = ☐

23 132 ÷ 12 = ☐

24 84 ÷ 12 = ☐

25 ☐ × 12 = 72

26 ☐ × 12 = 12

27 ☐ × 12 = 144

28 ☐ × 12 = 96

29 ☐ × 12 = 24

30 ☐ × 12 = 84

31 ☐ × 12 = 60

32 ☐ × 12 = 132

33 ☐ × 12 = 36

34 ☐ × 12 = 120

35 ☐ × 12 = 96

36 ☐ × 12 = 48

37 ☐ ÷ 12 = 10

38 ☐ ÷ 12 = 5

39 ☐ ÷ 12 = 7

40 ☐ ÷ 12 = 0

41 ☐ ÷ 12 = 3

42 ☐ ÷ 12 = 8

43 ☐ ÷ 12 = 12

44 ☐ ÷ 12 = 4

45 ☐ ÷ 12 = 9

46 ☐ ÷ 12 = 2

47 ☐ ÷ 12 = 6

48 ☐ ÷ 12 = 11

Write down the area and perimeter for each shape.

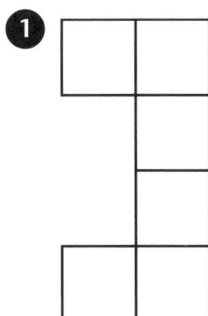

1

Area ☐ cm²   Perim. ☐ cm

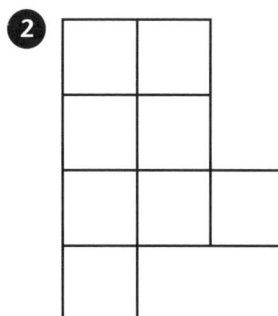

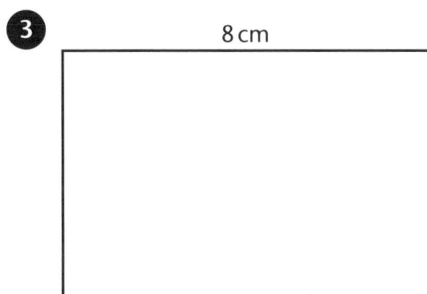

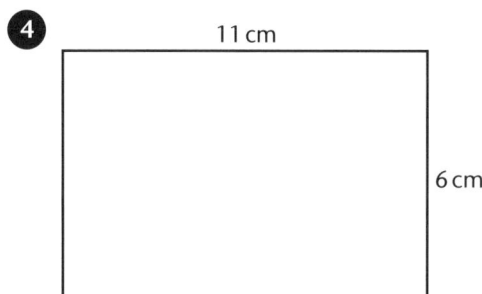

2

Area ☐ cm²   Perim. ☐ cm

3

8 cm

5 cm

Area ☐ cm²   Perim. ☐ cm

4

11 cm

6 cm

Area ☐ cm²   Perim. ☐ cm

Write the missing measurements for each shape.

5 square

sides   7 cm

Area   ....

Perim.   ....

6 rectangle

sides 5 cm, 3 cm

Area   ....

Perim.   ....

7 square

sides   ....

Area   ....

Perim. 40 cm

8 rectangle

sides 15 cm, ...

Area   60 cm²

Perim.   ....

9 Fill in the missing measurements

Length (cm)	Width (cm)	Area (cm²)	Perimeter (cm)
10	4		
7	2		
14	5		
9			36
20		200	
	8		40

10 Draw a rectangle with a length of 3·5 cm and a perimeter of 12 cm. Label the width measurement.

1 This table shows the weight of the 360 children in a Junior School.

Weight (kg)	Number of children
21–25	40
26–30	65
31–35	90
36–40	85
41–45	55
46–50	35

Use the grid to draw an horizontal bar chart labelled in tens. Remember to label the axes.

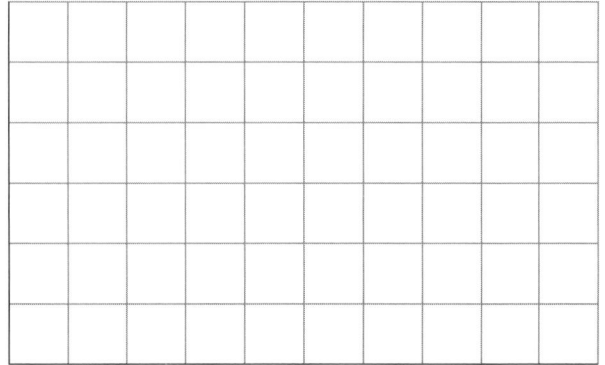

2 This table shows the time taken by children to travel to their Secondary School.

Time (minutes)	Number of children
1–10	120
11–20	150
21–30	180
31–40	90
41–50	65
51–60	50
Over 60	10

Use the grid to draw a vertical bar chart labelled in 20s. Remember to label the axes.

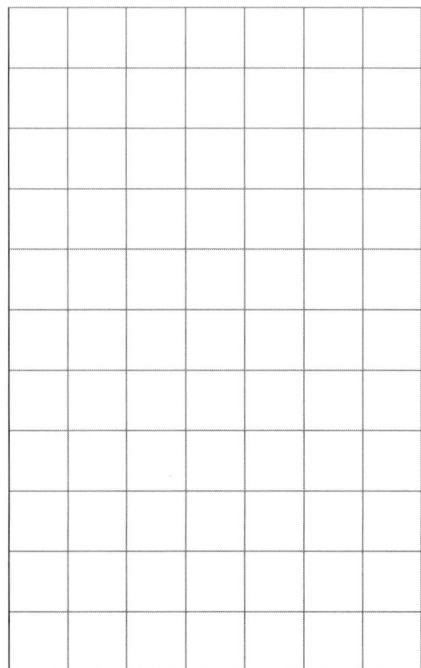

The table shows the marks achieved by six Secondary School pupils in their end of year exams.

Subject	Ashley	Bina	Calvin	Deva	Errol	Fran
Maths	72	34	57	91	67	42
English	58	81	66	40	54	72
Science	35	75	82	69	93	59
History	86	48	95	84	75	38
Geography	40	93	67	35	45	90
Art	69	52	34	75	56	85
IT	93	78	49	52	80	46
Music	45	61	75	88	34	65

1 Who had the highest mark in Geography? ....

2 What was the lowest mark in IT? ....

3 What mark was scored by Errol in English? ....

4 Who scored 75 in Art? ....

5 In which subject did Ashley score 45? ....

6 Who scored 15 more than Fran in Maths? ....

7 How many pupils scored more than 65 in Music? ....

8 Which children scored more than 55 in:

   a) English ....

   b) Art? ....

9 Which subject had the smallest difference between top mark and bottom mark? ....

10 Who had a total mark for all eight subjects of 534? ....

   HINT. Find the total of the units column.

   Does it end in 4?

11 When the marks of six pupils are combined which subject had the highest total mark?

   HINT. Find the total of the tens digits. ....

Examples $\frac{5}{6}$ of 180 m = (180 m ÷ 6) × 5 $\frac{3}{10}$ of £450 = (£450 ÷ 10) × 3

$= 30\,\text{m} \times 5$ $= £45 \times 3$

$= 150\,\text{m}$ $= £135$

Find

1 $\frac{1}{10}$ of 800 g   ....

2 $\frac{3}{10}$ of 800 g   ....

3 $\frac{7}{10}$ of 800 g   ....

4 $\frac{1}{5}$ of 200 m   ....

5 $\frac{2}{5}$ of 200 m   ....

6 $\frac{4}{5}$ of 200 m   ....

7 $\frac{1}{8}$ of 400 ml   ....

8 $\frac{2}{8}$ of 400 ml   ....

9 $\frac{5}{8}$ of 400 ml   ....

10 $\frac{1}{100}$ of £1500   ....

11 $\frac{4}{100}$ of £1500   ....

12 $\frac{20}{100}$ of £1500   ....

Find

13 $\frac{1}{2}$ of £140   ....

14 $\frac{1}{10}$ of 250 g   ....

15 $\frac{1}{4}$ of 36p   ....

16 $\frac{1}{7}$ of 350 m   ....

17 $\frac{1}{3}$ of 18 litres   ....

18 $\frac{1}{11}$ of 132 km   ....

19 $\frac{1}{6}$ of 48 cm   ....

20 $\frac{1}{12}$ of 360 kg   ....

21 $\frac{3}{4}$ of 240 ml   ....

22 $\frac{4}{9}$ of £72   ....

23 $\frac{5}{6}$ of 30 mm   ....

24 $\frac{9}{10}$ of 500 g   ....

25 $\frac{3}{5}$ of 60p   ....

26 $\frac{2}{3}$ of 27 kg   ....

27 $\frac{3}{8}$ of 880 m   ....

28 $\frac{5}{12}$ of 48 litres   ....

Using fractions count from 0 to 1 in steps of:

1 one fifth ....

2 one ninth ....

3 one eighth ....

4 one twelfth ....

Using fractions count back from 1 to 0 in steps of:

5 one quarter ....

6 one sixth ....

7 one tenth ....

8 one seventh ....

Write the first six steps in each sequence.

Using decimals count on:

9 in tenths from 5·5 ....

10 in hundredths from 0 ....

11 in tenths from 0·83 ....

12 in hundredths from 1·76. ....

Using decimals count back:

13 in tenths from 2·5 ....

14 in hundredths from 1·7 ....

15 in tenths from 4·19 ....

16 in hundredths from 3. ....

Write the missing number in the box. Show your calculations and conversions.

1 Gerry lives 1·2 km from school.
Judy lives 560 m nearer school.

Judy lives ☐ m from school.

1·2 km = 1200 m

1200 − 560 = ...

6 Des cuts six 15 cm lengths from a
5 m ball of string.

He cuts off ☐ m altogether.

2 Bottles of water hold 250 ml.

Six bottles hold ☐ litres.

7 A parcel weighs 2·6 kg.
Another parcel is 850 g heavier.

This parcel weighs ☐ kg.

3 Lisa is 1·33 m tall.
Her father is 49 cm taller.

Lisa's father is ☐ m tall.

8 A pile of 5 dictionaries is 14 cm tall.

Each dictionary is ☐ cm thick.

4 10 bricks weigh 8 kg altogether.

One brick weighs ☐ g.

9 Four 300 ml mugs are filled with water
from a kettle holding 2·75 litres.

☐ litres is left in the kettle.

5 Vikram has £4·37.
He spends 85p.

He has £ ☐ left.

10 Sophie buys eight 30p cards.

She spends £ ☐ altogether.

Write the missing number in the box.

1 A newspaper costs 60p.

Seven papers cost £ ☐ altogether.

7 Drinks cost 55p each.
Maia buys three for £1·20

She saves ☐ p.

2 Gilda buys apples for 79p and oranges for 94p.

She spends £ ☐ altogether.

8 Neville has five 50p coins and nine 20p coins.

He has £ ☐ altogether.

3 Six eggs cost £1·20 altogether.

One egg costs ☐ p.

9 Drew buys a card for £1·60 and a present for £12·95. He pays £20.

He receives £ ☐ change.

4 Malcolm pays for shopping with a £10 note and receives 87p change.

His shopping costs £ ☐ .

10 A scarf costs £7·50. One tenth is taken off the price.

The new price is £ ☐ .

5 Yogurts cost 45p each.

Four yogurts cost £ ☐ altogether.

11 4 drinks cost the same as 3 cakes.
Drinks cost 60p each.

Cakes cost £ ☐ each.

6 Pencils cost 49p.
Pens cost 76p more than pencils.

Pens cost £ ☐ .

12 Lollies cost 90p each.
Ice creams cost 80p each.

Three lollies and two ice creams

cost £ ☐ altogether.

Show your working. Write the answer in the box.

1 Green apples 5748
Red apples 3293

[   ] apples altogether

2 Each glass holds 185 ml.

Six glasses hold [   ] ml.

3 A new car costs £9168.
A used car costs £4795.

The used car is £[   ] cheaper.

4 9 flowers in each tray

[   ] trays for 603 flowers

5 12 rolls in each pack

[   ] rolls in 279 packs

6 Saturday 4370 shoppers

Sunday [   ] shoppers

1536 fewer shoppers on Sunday.

7 coach fare £8
passengers 57

total of fares £[   ]

8 fiction books 3569
non-fiction books 1847

total number of books [   ]

The Ancient Romans used letters to stand for numbers.

Roman Numerals	I	V	X	L	C
Arabic Numerals	1	5	10	50	100

Write as Arabic numerals.

1 XLVIII ....

2 LXXXVII ....

3 XXIX ....

4 XCVI ....

5 XV ....

6 LX ....

7 XXXIV ....

8 LI ....

9 VIII ....

10 LXXIX ....

11 XLIII ....

12 LXXX ....

13 XXVI ....

14 XCVII ....

15 XIX ....

16 LXIV ....

17 XXXI ....

18 LV ....

19 IV ....

20 LXXII ....

21 XLVIII ....

22 XVII ....

23 XXIII ....

24 XCIX ....

Write as Roman numerals.

25 35 ....

26 28 ....

27 90 ....

28 56 ....

29 83 ....

30 44 ....

31 12 ....

32 9 ....

33 77 ....

34 24 ....

35 81 ....

36 39 ....

37 66 ....

38 93 ....

39 58 ....

40 42 ....

41 6 ....

42 20 ....

43 75 ....

44 84 ....

45 37 ....

46 59 ....

47 63 ....

48 98 ....

Writing the missing number in the box.

1 35 + 38 = ☐

2 68 + 23 = ☐

3 49 + ☐ = 86

4 26 + ☐ = 62

5 ☐ + 17 = 95

6 ☐ + 59 = 80

7 76 + 48 = ☐

8 47 + 54 = ☐

9 94 + ☐ = 143

10 69 + ☐ = 135

11 ☐ + 27 = 112

12 ☐ + 52 = 150

13 76 + 57 = ☐

14 93 + 29 = ☐

15 67 + ☐ = 164

16 59 + ☐ = 117

17 ☐ + 66 = 141

18 ☐ + 38 = 105

19 51 − 22 = ☐

20 92 − 37 = ☐

21 75 − ☐ = 46

22 83 − ☐ = 68

23 ☐ − 29 = 38

24 ☐ − 45 = 49

25 113 − 34 = ☐

26 131 − 45 = ☐

27 126 − ☐ = 68

28 170 − ☐ = 97

29 ☐ − 29 = 73

30 ☐ − 56 = 88

31 154 − 67 = ☐

32 138 − 39 = ☐

33 110 − ☐ = 66

34 161 − ☐ = 88

35 ☐ − 88 = 94

36 ☐ − 36 = 87

Write the missing number in the box.

1 8 × 6 = ☐   **4** ☐ × 10 = 90   **7** ☐ ÷ 8 = 6

2 6 × 5 = ☐   **5** ☐ × 7 = 84   **8** ☐ ÷ 2 = 9

3 12 × 9 = ☐   **6** ☐ × 6 = 42   **9** ☐ ÷ 7 = 8

10 7 × 12 = ☐   **13** ☐ × 4 = 32   **16** ☐ ÷ 5 = 1

11 6 × 7 = ☐   **14** ☐ × 12 = 132   **17** ☐ ÷ 9 = 7

12 9 × 3 = ☐   **15** ☐ × 8 = 56   **18** ☐ ÷ 6 = 6

19 11 × 8 = ☐   **22** ☐ × 9 = 81   **25** ☐ ÷ 11 = 11

20 7 × 4 = ☐   **23** ☐ × 3 = 36   **26** ☐ ÷ 12 = 12

21 12 × 6 = ☐   **24** ☐ × 7 = 49   **27** ☐ ÷ 8 = 8

28 0 × 11 = ☐   **31** ☐ × 5 = 60   **34** ☐ ÷ 4 = 6

29 5 × 9 = ☐   **32** ☐ × 6 = 54   **35** ☐ ÷ 7 = 5

30 4 × 12 = ☐   **33** ☐ × 12 = 96   **36** ☐ ÷ 9 = 8

37 11 × 2 = ☐   **40** ☐ × 11 = 11   **43** ☐ ÷ 6 = 11

38 9 × 7 = ☐   **41** ☐ × 8 = 72   **44** ☐ ÷ 3 = 7

39 12 × 8 = ☐   **42** ☐ × 9 = 54   **45** ☐ ÷ 12 = 9

Write the missing numbers.

1 $45 \times 7 = 40 \times 7 + 5 \times 7$

$= \underline{280} + \underline{35}$

$= \underline{}$

2 $38 \times 3 = 30 \times 3 + 8 \times 3$

$= \underline{90} + \underline{}$

$= \underline{}$

3 $79 \times 2 = \underline{} + \underline{}$

$= \underline{} + \underline{}$

$= \underline{}$

4 $26 \times 8 = \underline{} + \underline{}$

$= \underline{} + \underline{}$

$= \underline{}$

Write the missing numbers.

5 $73 \times 6 = 420 + 18$

$= \underline{}$

6 $47 \times 4 = 160 + \underline{}$

$= \underline{}$

7 $35 \times 9 = \underline{} + 45$

$= \underline{}$

8 $29 \times 7 = \underline{} + \underline{}$

$= \underline{}$

9 $56 \times 5 = \underline{} + \underline{}$

$= \underline{}$

10 $87 \times 8 = \underline{} + \underline{}$

$= \underline{}$

11 $25 \times 6 = \underline{} + \underline{}$

$= \underline{}$

12 $68 \times 9 = \underline{} + \underline{}$

$= \underline{}$

Work out

13 86×2 $\underline{}$

14 74×7 $\underline{}$

15 49×6 $\underline{}$

16 35×8 $\underline{}$

17 57×3 $\underline{}$

18 94×9 $\underline{}$

19 68×7 $\underline{}$

20 49×5 $\underline{}$

21 86×6 $\underline{}$

22 39×4 $\underline{}$

23 94×8 $\underline{}$

24 27×9 $\underline{}$

> *Examples* $\dfrac{5}{8} + \dfrac{2}{8} = \dfrac{7}{8}$ $\dfrac{5}{8} + \dfrac{4}{8} = 9$ eighths = 1 and $\dfrac{1}{8}$
>
> $\dfrac{7}{10} - \dfrac{4}{10} = \dfrac{3}{10}$ $\dfrac{7}{10} + \dfrac{7}{10} = 14$ tenths = 1 and $\dfrac{4}{10}$

Write the missing numbers in the boxes.

1 $\dfrac{4}{10} + \dfrac{2}{10} = \boxed{\dfrac{\ }{\ }}$

2 $\dfrac{2}{4} + \dfrac{1}{4} = \boxed{\dfrac{\ }{\ }}$

3 $\dfrac{3}{7} + \dfrac{1}{7} = \boxed{\dfrac{\ }{\ }}$

4 $1 - \dfrac{2}{3} = \boxed{\dfrac{\ }{\ }}$

5 $\dfrac{8}{11} - \dfrac{6}{11} = \boxed{\dfrac{\ }{\ }}$

6 $\dfrac{7}{8} - \dfrac{2}{8} = \boxed{\dfrac{\ }{\ }}$

7 $\dfrac{2}{5} + \boxed{\ } = \dfrac{4}{5}$

8 $\dfrac{5}{12} + \boxed{\ } = \dfrac{8}{12}$

9 $\dfrac{3}{6} + \boxed{\ } = \dfrac{5}{6}$

10 $\dfrac{8}{9} - \boxed{\ } = \dfrac{4}{9}$

11 $1 - \boxed{\ } = \dfrac{3}{4}$

12 $\dfrac{9}{10} - \boxed{\ } = \dfrac{6}{10}$

13 $\boxed{\ } + \dfrac{3}{8} = \dfrac{6}{8}$

14 $\boxed{\ } + \dfrac{1}{3} = \dfrac{2}{3}$

15 $\boxed{\ } + \dfrac{2}{9} = \dfrac{7}{9}$

16 $\boxed{\ } - \dfrac{5}{12} = \dfrac{4}{12}$

17 $\boxed{\ } - \dfrac{3}{5} = \dfrac{1}{5}$

18 $\boxed{\ } - \dfrac{1}{6} = \dfrac{5}{6}$

Write the missing number in the box.

19 $\boxed{\ }$ fifths $= \dfrac{4}{5} + \dfrac{3}{5}$

20 $\boxed{\ }$ eighths $= \dfrac{7}{8} + \dfrac{4}{8}$

21 $\boxed{\ }$ sixths $= \dfrac{5}{6} + \dfrac{5}{6}$

22 4 thirds $= \dfrac{\boxed{\ }}{3} + \dfrac{2}{3}$

23 13 twelfths $= \dfrac{9}{12} + \dfrac{\boxed{\ }}{12}$

24 12 ninths $= \dfrac{7}{9} + \boxed{\dfrac{\ }{\ }}$

25 1 and $\dfrac{1}{4} = \dfrac{3}{4} + \boxed{\dfrac{\ }{\ }}$

26 1 and $\dfrac{4}{7} = \dfrac{6}{7} + \boxed{\dfrac{\ }{\ }}$

27 1 and $\dfrac{5}{12} = \dfrac{11}{12} + \boxed{\dfrac{\ }{\ }}$

28 1 and $\boxed{\dfrac{\ }{\ }} = \dfrac{5}{10} + \dfrac{8}{10}$

29 1 and $\boxed{\dfrac{\ }{\ }} = \dfrac{3}{8} + \dfrac{6}{8}$

30 1 and $\boxed{\dfrac{\ }{\ }} = \dfrac{7}{11} + \dfrac{8}{11}$

Round to the nearest:

pound	whole number	metre
1 £5·73	**7** 43·19	**13** 8·61 m ....
2 £12·45	**8** 1·81	**14** 16·39 m ....
3 £8·52	**9** 0·74	**15** 2·53 m ....
4 £56·90	**10** 74·26	**16** 89·47 m ....
5 £20·37	**11** 7·08	**17** 30·84 m ....
6 £9·64	**12** 25·92	**18** 3·25 m ....

Draw a circle around the larger of each pair of numbers.

19 0·23 0·3	**21** 6·4 4·66	**23** 3·12 3·2
20 9·78 8·97	**22** 1·05 0·54	**24** 2·5 2·25

25 Locate the letters on the line.

A 0·4   B 0·8   C 0·95   D 0·1   E 0·25   F 0·65

Arrange the decimals in order. Start with the smallest.

26 3·77   7·3   3·7   7·07   7   ....

27 5·56   5·6   6·5   0·66   6·06   ....

28 9·9   1·99   9·1   11·1   9·19   ....

29 4·2   2·24   4·02   2·4   0·44   ....

30 8·8   80·8   0·8   8·88   8·08   ....

Measure each shape and fill in the boxes to find the perimeter.

1

Length ☐ cm × 2 = ☐ cm

Width ☐ cm × 2 = ☐ cm

Perimeter = ☐ cm

2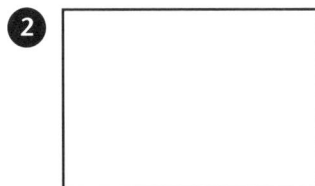

Length ☐ cm × 2 = ☐ cm

Width ☐ cm × 2 = ☐ cm

Perimeter = ☐ cm

Write the perimeter

3 square   sides 3·5 cm

perimeter = ☐ cm

4 rectangle   sides 9 cm 4 cm

perimeter = ☐ cm

5 hexagon   all sides 5 cm

perimeter = ☐ cm

6 Complete this table showing the measurements of rectangles.

Length	Width	Perimeter
6 cm	1·2 cm	
12 cm	10 cm	
5 m	4·5 m	
7·5 m	6 m	
2·8 cm	1·6 cm	
4·3 cm	2·5 cm	

For each shape find the missing lengths and work out the perimeter.
All lengths are in centimetres.

7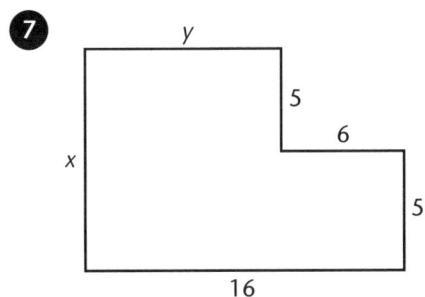

8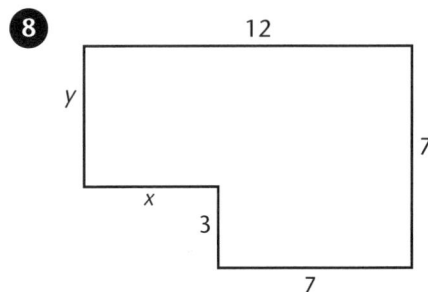

x ☐ cm y ☐ cm perimeter ☐ cm x ☐ cm y ☐ cm perimeter ☐ cm

Examples

760 ml + ☐ = 1 litre (1000 ml)

760 → 800 = 40

800 → 1000 = 200

Answer 240 ml

70 g × 60 = ☐ kg

70 × 60 = 4200

4200 g = 4·2 kg

Answer 4·2 kg

Work out mentally.

1 62 cm + ☐ cm = 1 m

2 19 cm + ☐ cm = 1 m

3 450 g + ☐ g = 1 kg

4 930 g + ☐ g = 1 kg

5 1 litre − ☐ ml = 810 ml

6 1 litre − ☐ ml = 280 ml

7 1 km − ☐ m = 340 m

8 1 km − ☐ m = 570 m

9 50 cm × 9 = ☐ m

10 6 cm × 40 = ☐ m

11 200 g × 7 = ☐ kg

12 80 g × 30 = ☐ kg

13 3·2 litres ÷ 8 = ☐ ml

14 1·4 litres ÷ 20 = ☐ ml

15 5·4 km ÷ 6 = ☐ m

16 4 km ÷ 50 = ☐ m

17 750 ml + ☐ ml = 1 litre

18 990 ml + ☐ ml = 1 litre

19 420 m + ☐ m = 1 km

20 660 m + ☐ m = 1 km

21 1 m − ☐ cm = 35 cm

22 1 m − ☐ cm = 87 cm

23 1 kg − ☐ g = 710 g

24 1 kg − ☐ g = 580 g

25 600 ml × 5 = ☐ litres

26 70 ml × 60 = ☐ litres

27 900 m × 2 = ☐ km

28 80 m × 80 = ☐ km

29 3·5 m ÷ 7 = ☐ cm

30 1·8 m ÷ 30 = ☐ cm

31 2·8 kg ÷ 4 = ☐ g

32 7·2 kg ÷ 90 = ☐ g

Sketch the reflection of each shape in the mirror line.

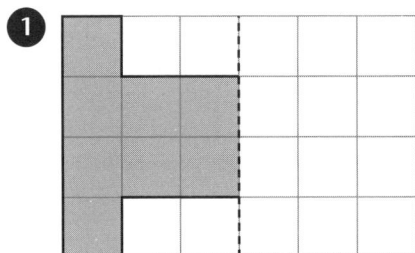

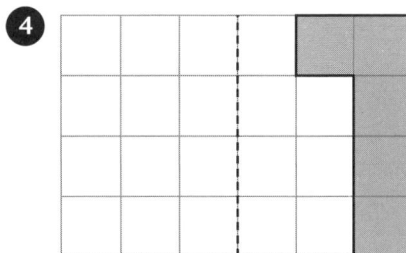

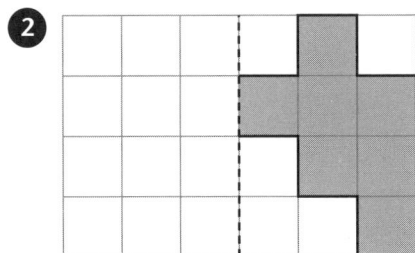

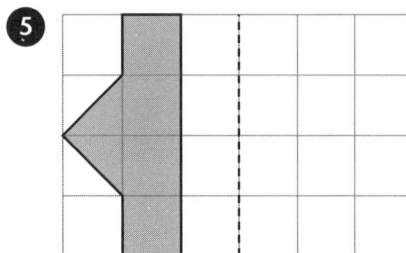

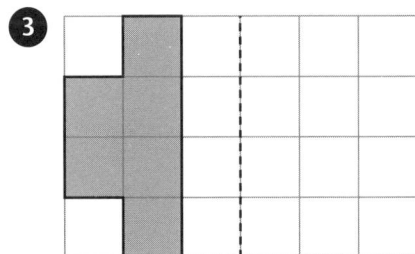

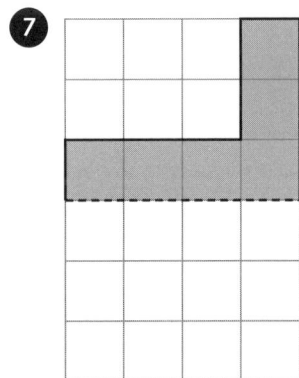

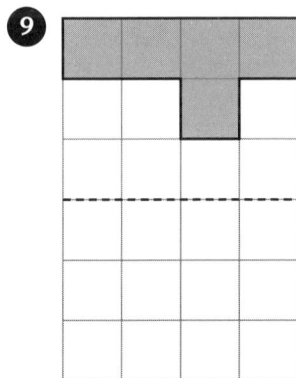

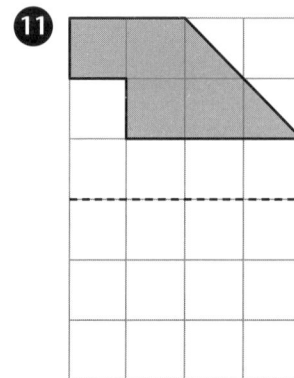

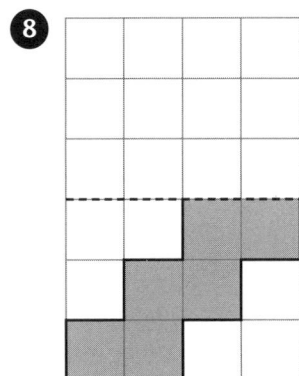

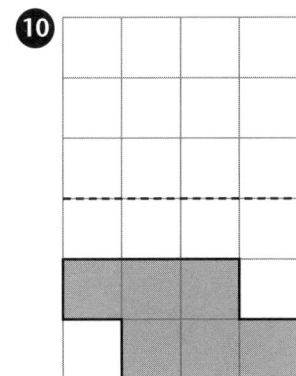

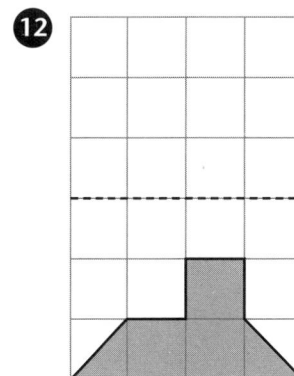

Plot the points and join them up in the order given to form a quadrilateral. Identify the shape.

1

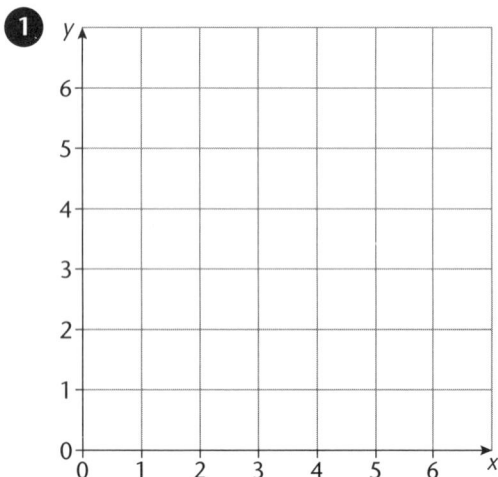

(2, 1) (4, 5) (6, 4) (4, 0) (2, 1)

The shape is a

....

3

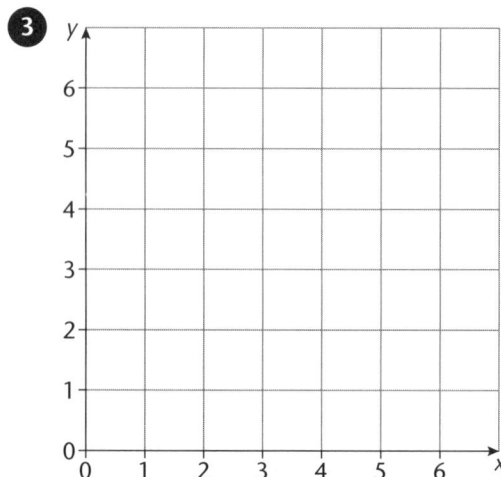

(0, 1) (2, 3) (6, 2) (4, 0) (0, 1)

The shape is a

....

2

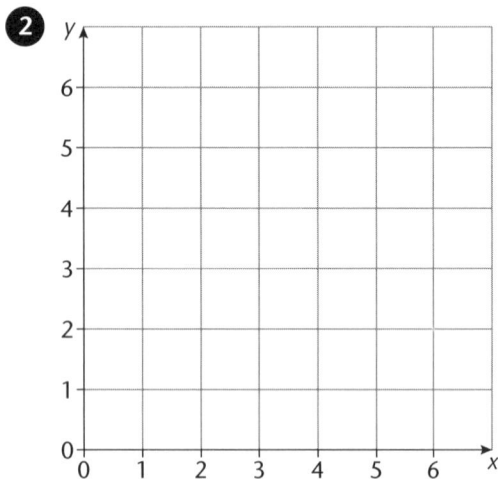

(1, 2) (0, 6) (4, 5) (5, 1) (1, 2)

The shape is a

....

4

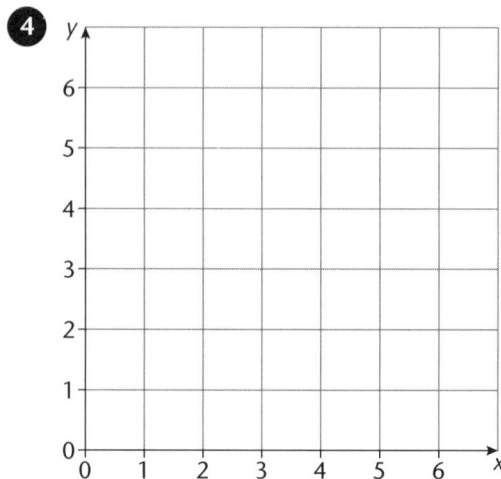

(1, 3) (3, 6) (6, 4) (4, 1) (1, 3)

The shape is a

....

Translate each shape as shown. Give the co-ordinates of the new position.

1 Right 3 Up 1

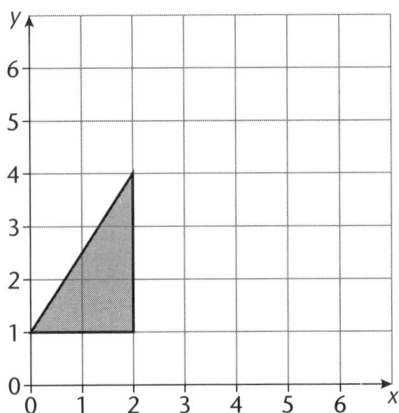

...(3, 2)...

....

....

4 Right 2 Down 2

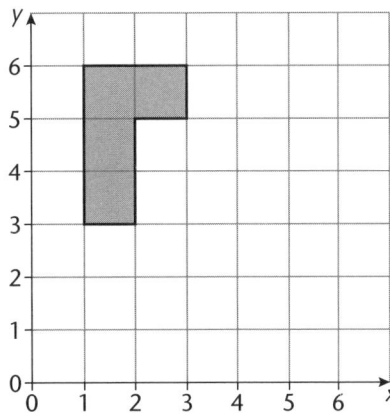

....

....

....

....

....

....

2 Left 2 Down 2

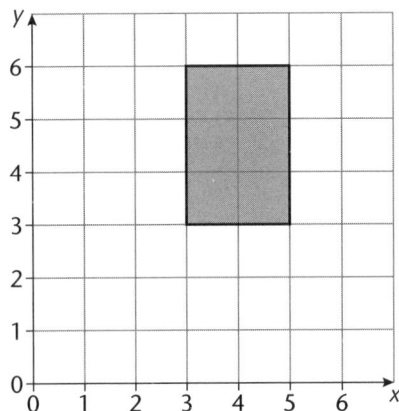

....

....

....

....

5 Right 4 Up 2

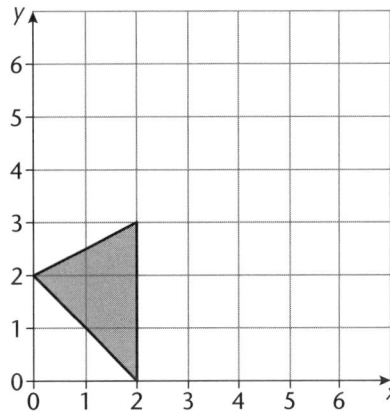

....

....

....

3 Left 3 Up 4

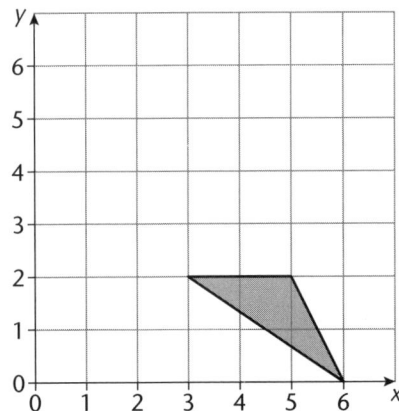

....

....

....

6 Left 2 Down 3

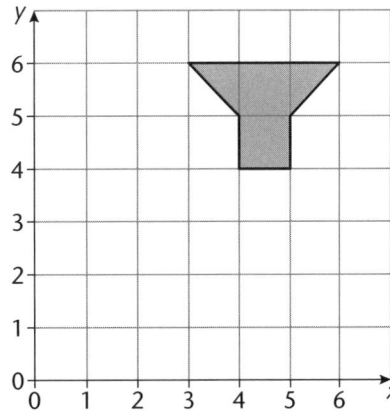

....

....

....

....

....

....

```
                                      5  14 15  1
  Examples        3 6 9 4            6̸ 5̸ 6̸ 0
                 + 2 3 8 7          − 1 7 6 9
                  ─────────          ─────────
                   6 0 8 1            4 7 9 1
                   ─────────          ─────────
                   1 1 1
```

Work out

1   3 7 5 8
      + 1 3 8 4
      ─────────

2   5 2 9 6
      + 2 7 2 4
      ─────────

3   4 4 8 7
      + 1 6 9 8
      ─────────

4   2 6 4 0
      − 1 1 8 2
      ─────────

5   7 5 8 7
      − 3 9 3 8
      ─────────

6   6 3 1 9
      − 5 7 5 4
      ─────────

7   3 9 6 5
      + 2 6 8 7
      ─────────

8   2 5 3 9
      + 1 5 8 4
      ─────────

9   3 8 9 4
      + 3 5 7 8
      ─────────

10   8 2 5 6
      − 4 7 0 9
      ─────────

11   3 4 1 7
      − 2 6 6 3
      ─────────

12   5 8 5 3
      − 3 2 7 4
      ─────────

13   5 6 5 7
      + 1 5 9 4
      ─────────

14   4 7 8 3
      + 3 5 7 9
      ─────────

15   2 4 6 8
      + 2 5 9 6
      ─────────

16   4 9 3 2
      − 1 7 6 5
      ─────────

17   9 6 0 7
      − 3 6 4 6
      ─────────

18   7 1 5 4
      − 2 8 4 9
      ─────────

Examples	479	47
	× 6	8)3 7⁵6
	2 8 7 4	
	₄ ₅	

Work out

1
```
    3 4 8
×       8
_____
```

5
```
    2 9 6
×       7
_____
```

9
```
    5 6 9
×       8
_____
```

2
```
    5 7 9
×       2
_____
```

6
```
    6 4 7
×       3
_____
```

10
```
    7 5 6
×       4
_____
```

3
```
    7 2 5
×       9
_____
```

7
```
    4 8 5
×       6
_____
```

11
```
    4 8 3
×       9
_____
```

4
```
    3 8 2
×     1 1
_____
```

8
```
    3 7 4
×       5
_____
```

12
```
    5 3 7
×     1 2
_____
```

13   5)3 2 5

17   3)1 7 7

21   4)3 3 6

14   6)2 2 2

18   9)8 6 4

22   6)5 7 0

15   2)1 7 2

19   12)4 5 6

23   11)5 1 7

16   7)2 6 6

20   8)2 1 6

24   7)3 9 9

Write the missing number in the box.

1   3 hours | 180 | minutes   9   120 minutes | | hours

2   $1\frac{1}{4}$ hours | | minutes   10   90 minutes | | hours

3   4 minutes | | seconds   11   180 seconds | | minutes

4   $2\frac{1}{2}$ minutes | | seconds   12   30 seconds | | minutes

5   6 years | | months   13   48 months | | years

6   $\frac{3}{4}$ year | | months   14   30 months | | years

7   10 weeks | | days   15   35 days | | weeks

8   4 weeks | | days   16   21 days | | weeks

How many minutes are left in the hour?   How many hours are left in the day?

17   quarter to | | 21   10 pm | |

18   25 past | | 22   4 am | |

19   3:35 | | 23   1 pm | |

20   2:05 | | 24   9 am | |

Write the date one week before:

25   June 16th   ....

26   September 4th   ....

Write the date two weeks after:

27   January 17th   ....

28   November 22nd   ....

Write the missing time or number in the box.

1 A lesson starts at 1:35. It finishes at 2:15. It lasts [ ] minutes.

7 The washing machine was switched on at 9:47. The wash lasted 36 minutes. It finished at [ ].

2 It is 6:43. There is 25 minutes before the train is due to leave. The train leaves at [ ].

8 The boat trip began at 12:30. It finished at 1:28. It lasted [ ] minutes.

3 At 4:15 Silas caught his first fish. He had been fishing 39 minutes. He started fishing at [ ].

9 A pie needs to be baked for 45 minutes. It is put into the oven at 4:51. It should be taken out at [ ].

4 Gwenda entered a shop at 11:45. She left at 12:02. She had been in the shop for [ ] minutes.

10 Jamila needs to be at work at 8:00. Her journey takes 22 minutes. The latest she can leave home is [ ].

5 Duncan swam for 43 minutes. He got out of the pool at 3:11. He had started swimming at [ ].

11 A TV programme begins at 3:25. It lasts 55 minutes. It ends at [ ].

6 A clock is 15 minutes slow. It shows 4:57. The actual time is [ ].

12 Karen begins her homework at 4:45. She finishes at 5: 17. It has taken her [ ] minutes.

This bar chart shows the number of blouses sold in a shop.

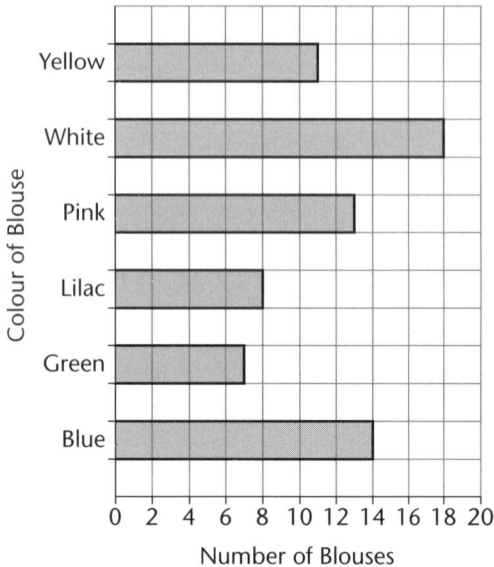

1 Which colour blouse was bought:

a) most often   ....

b) least often?   ....

2 Which colour blouse was bought:

a) by 8 people   ....

b) by 13 people?   ....

3 How many people bought:

a) a blue blouse   ....

b) a yellow blouse?   ....

4 How many more people bought a white blouse than a yellow blouse?

                                 ....

5 How many fewer people bought a green blouse than a blue blouse?

                                 ....

6 How many blouses were sold altogether?

                                 ....

This bar chart shows the total sales of a shop in six days.

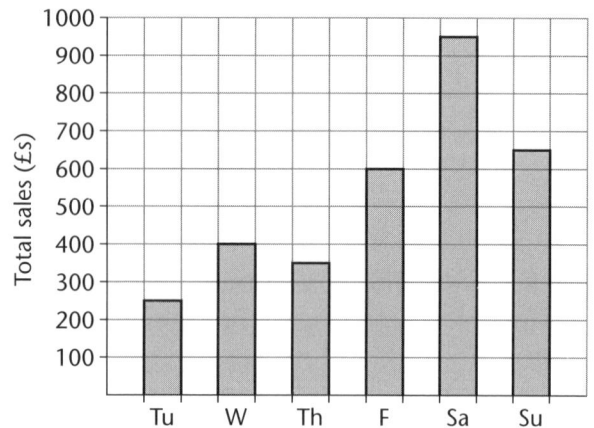

7 What were the total sales on:

a) Wednesday   ....

b) Sunday?   ....

8 On which day were total sales:

a) highest   ....

b) lowest   ....

c) £600   ....

d) £350?   ....

9 How much larger were total sales on Saturday than Sunday?

                                 ....

10 How much smaller were total sales on Tuesday than Wednesday?

                                 ....

11 What were the total sales:

a) at the weekend   ....

b) during the six days?   ....

This graph shows the average daily maximum temperature recorded in New York for one year.

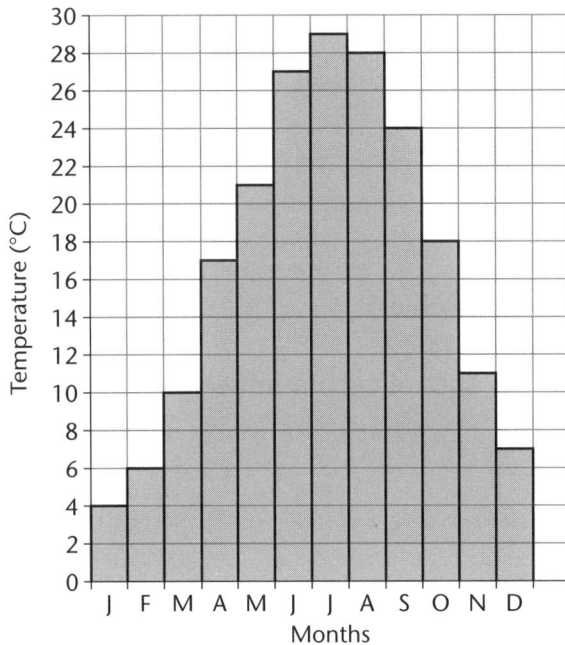

This graph shows the cost of family holidays sold by a Travel Agency.

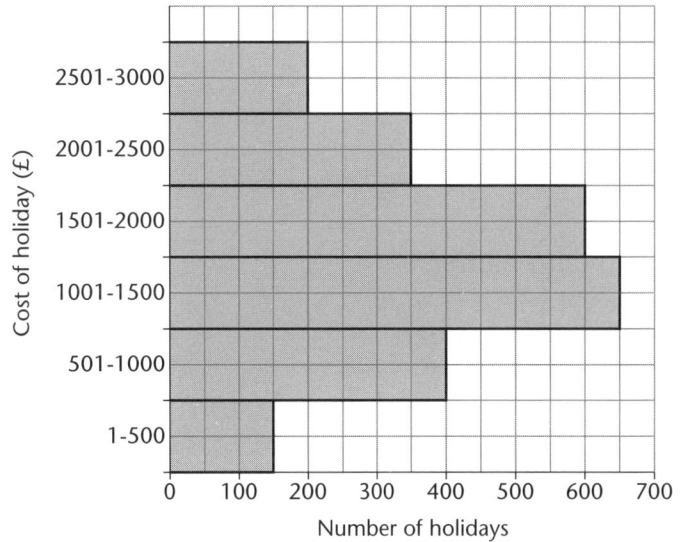

1 What was the temperature in:

a) August   ....

b) December?   ....

2 In which month was the temperature:

a) 6°C   ....

b) 27°C?   ....

3 How much higher was the temperature in July than January?   ....

4 How much lower was the temperature in May than June?   ....

5 Between which two months was there the largest:

a) rise in temperature

....

b) fall in temperature?

....

6 How many holidays were sold for between:

a) £2501 and £3000   ....

b) £1001 and £1500?   ....

7 Which price range was bought by:

a) 400 people   ....

b) 350 people?   ....

8 How many holidays were bought for:

a) £1000 or less   ....

b) more than £2000?   ....

9 How many more holidays were bought for £1001–£1500 than £1501–£2000?

....

10 How many fewer holidays were bought for £1–£500 than £501–£1000?

....

11 How many more holidays were bought for £1–£1500 than £1501–£3000?

....

12 How many holidays were bought altogether?   ....

Find the number.

1 a 2-digit number
a multiple of 9
the sum of its digits is 18

  The number is ....

2 a 3-digit number
a multiple of 11
the sum of its digits is 8

  The number is ....

Find both numbers.

3 2-digit numbers
multiples of 7
the sum of each number is 10

  Answer .... and ....

4 2-digit numbers
multiples of 12
the product of each numbers digits is 32

  Answer .... and ....

Find three consecutive numbers with a total of:

5 15   ....

6 27   ....

7 60   ....

8 111   ....

Find two consecutive numbers with a product of:

9 20   ....

10 42   ....

11 110   ....

12 56   ....

Fill in the missing numbers.

13 $25 - 9 = 12 + \boxed{}$

14 $10 + \boxed{} = 30 - 8$

15 $8 + 4 = \boxed{} - 12$

16 $\boxed{} - 21 = 18 + 7$

17 $2 \times \boxed{} + 8 = 18$

18 $\boxed{} \div 3 - 5 = 4$

19 $7 \times \boxed{} - 16 = 40$

20 $\boxed{} \div 12 + 5 = 10$

Examples $\frac{1}{8}$ of 40 kg = 40 kg ÷ 8

= 5 kg

$\frac{3}{8}$ of 40 kg = ($\frac{1}{8}$ of 40 kg) × 3

= 5 kg × 3

= 15 kg

Find

1 $\frac{1}{4}$ of 28 mm ....

2 $\frac{3}{4}$ of 28 mm ....

3 $\frac{1}{4}$ of £40 ....

4 $\frac{3}{4}$ of £40 ....

5 $\frac{1}{10}$ of 60 m ....

6 $\frac{7}{10}$ of 60 m ....

7 $\frac{1}{10}$ of 500 ml ....

8 $\frac{9}{10}$ of 500 ml ....

9 $\frac{1}{5}$ of 20 kg ....

10 $\frac{2}{5}$ of 20 kg ....

11 $\frac{1}{5}$ of 45p ....

12 $\frac{4}{5}$ of 45p ....

Work out

13 $\frac{7}{10}$ of 60 cm ....

14 $\frac{3}{8}$ of 24 kg ....

15 $\frac{2}{7}$ of 35p ....

16 $\frac{5}{100}$ of 200 mm ....

17 $\frac{1}{2}$ of 50 g ....

18 $\frac{4}{5}$ of £30 ....

19 $\frac{3}{4}$ of 20p ....

20 $\frac{1}{6}$ of 48 km ....

21 $\frac{3}{10}$ of 200 g ....

22 $\frac{7}{8}$ of 80 cm ....

23 $\frac{2}{9}$ of 36 kg ....

24 $\frac{5}{100}$ of £1000 ....

25 $\frac{3}{5}$ of 50 g ....

26 $\frac{11}{12}$ of 48 cm ....

27 $\frac{2}{3}$ of 18p ....

28 $\frac{3}{4}$ of 48 m ....

29 $\frac{5}{8}$ of £32 ....

30 $\frac{9}{10}$ of 1000 ml ....

Write in words

1 5092 ....

2 2708 ....

Write in order, starting with the smallest.

3 3434   3344   4333   3433   ....

4 6688   6886   6808   6680   ....

Give the value of the underlined digit.

5 71<u>5</u>9 ....   **6** 3<u>8</u>46 ....   **7** <u>2</u>098 ....   **8** 54<u>3</u>2 ....

Work out.

9 2791 + 10 ....   **11** 5642 + 100 ....

10 4836 − 10 ....   **12** 8097 − 100 ....

Round to the nearest:

(100)   (1000)

	Write as Roman numerals.	Write as Arabic numbers.

13 5738 ....   **17** 35 ....   **21** LXIX ....

14 3282 ....   **18** 49 ....   **22** XXVII ....

15 1545 ....   **19** 72 ....   **23** LXXXIV ....

16 9653 ....   **20** 96 ....   **24** LVIII ....

Count on   Count back

25 four 9s from 27 ....   **29** 5 from 2 ....

26 six 1000s from 2138 ....   **30** 7 from 5 ....

27 five 6s from 50 ....   **31** 6 from 1 ....

28 seven 50s from 1200 ....   **32** 10 from 4 ....

Work out

1 90 + 40 ....

2 1500 − 800 ....

3 5712 + 500 ....

4 100 − 37 ....

5 2347 + 60 ....

6 1000 − 550 ....

7 78 + 45 ....

8 112 − 27 ....

9 95 + 79 ....

10 141 − 64 ....

Write the missing number in the box.

11 400 × 6 = ☐

12 270 ÷ 3 = ☐

13 500 × 0 = ☐

14 6300 ÷ 9 = ☐

15 60 × 12 = ☐

16 ☐ ÷ 5 = 400

17 ☐ × 8 = 720

18 ☐ ÷ 11 = 110

19 ☐ × 4 = 4800

20 ☐ ÷ 7 = 60

Work out

21
```
  5 2 7 4
+ 3 9 4 6
─────────
```

22
```
  7 1 3 6
− 5 9 7 4
─────────
```

23
```
    7 4 8
×       9
─────────
```

24
```
4)2 7 6
```

25
```
  3 6 9 5
+ 1 8 4 9
─────────
```

26
```
  4 5 8 0
− 1 7 3 6
─────────
```

27
```
    3 9 7
×       5
─────────
```

28
```
7)3 7 8
```

29
```
  4 8 3 7
+ 3 1 7 6
─────────
```

30
```
  8 2 4 5
− 3 6 4 9
─────────
```

31
```
    8 0 6
×       6
─────────
```

32
```
8)3 0 4
```

Complete the equivalent fractions.

1 $\frac{1}{4} = \frac{\square}{8}$

3 $\frac{5}{6} = \frac{\square}{12}$

5 $\frac{3}{4} = \frac{\square}{12}$

7 $\frac{4}{5} = \frac{\square}{10}$

2 $\frac{1}{3} = \frac{\square}{9}$

4 $\frac{1}{2} = \frac{\square}{10}$

6 $\frac{2}{3} = \frac{\square}{6}$

8 $\frac{1}{2} = \frac{\square}{8}$

Work out

9 $\frac{3}{8} + \frac{2}{8} = \frac{\square}{\square}$

10 $\frac{2}{5} + \frac{1}{5} = \frac{\square}{\square}$

11 $\frac{7}{12} + \frac{4}{12} = \frac{\square}{\square}$

12 $\frac{5}{6} - \frac{3}{6} = \frac{\square}{\square}$

13 $1 - \frac{2}{3} = \frac{\square}{\square}$

14 $\frac{9}{10} - \frac{5}{10} = \frac{\square}{\square}$

Work out

15 $\frac{1}{5}$ of 60   ....

16 $\frac{2}{3}$ of 21   ....

17 $\frac{5}{8}$ of 72   ....

18 $\frac{1}{10}$ of 600   ....

19 $\frac{7}{10}$ of 50   ....

20 $\frac{3}{100}$ of 2000   ....

Write as decimals

21 $\frac{27}{100}$ ....

22 $\frac{1}{2}$ ....

23 $\frac{6}{10}$ ....

24 $\frac{9}{100}$ ....

25 $\frac{3}{4}$ ....

26 $\frac{63}{100}$ ....

Divide by

(10)   (100)

27 36   ....

28 7   ....

29 20   ....

30 85   ....

31 53   ....

32 90   ....

33 4   ....

34 68   ....

Give the value of the underlined figure in each number.

35 <u>2</u>·5   ....

36 6·0<u>9</u>   ....

37 31·<u>4</u>   ....

38 <u>9</u>0·37   ....

39 0·8<u>2</u>   ....

40 50·<u>6</u>   ....

41 14<u>7</u>·5   ....

42 4·1<u>8</u>   ....

Round to the nearest whole one.

43 3·9   ....

44 28·3   ....

45 36·5   ....

46 14·2   ....

47 71·7   ....

48 19·4   ....

49 80·6   ....

50 7·5   ....

Write the missing number in the box.

1 28 mm = ☐ cm

2 9 cm = ☐ m

3 465 cm = ☐ m

4 500 m = ☐ km

5 140 g = ☐ kg

6 3200 g = ☐ kg

7 80 ml = ☐ litres

8 1750 ml = ☐ litres

9 0·3 cm = ☐ mm

10 1·8 m = ☐ cm

11 0·57 m = ☐ cm

12 1·24 km = ☐ m

13 0·6 kg = ☐ g

14 2·13 kg = ☐ g

15 5·9 litres = ☐ ml

16 0·42 litres = ☐ ml

Find the area and perimeter for each shape.

17 rectangle   Area ☐ cm²

sides 7 cm, 4 cm   Perimeter ☐ cm

18 square   Area ☐ cm²

sides 12 cm   Perimeter ☐ cm

Write the missing measurements and perimeter (P). All lengths are in centimetres.

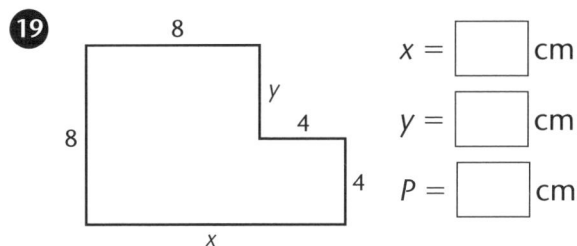

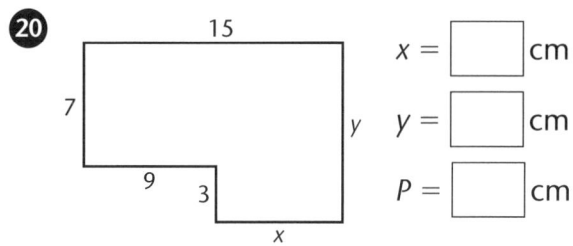

19

$x =$ ☐ cm

$y =$ ☐ cm

$P =$ ☐ cm

20

$x =$ ☐ cm

$y =$ ☐ cm

$P =$ ☐ cm

21 Write the equivalent 12-hour and 24-hour clock times.

12-HOUR	7:35 am	1:19 pm	2:43 am			
24-HOUR	07:35			18:27	05:51	23:04

Write the angles in order of size, smallest first.

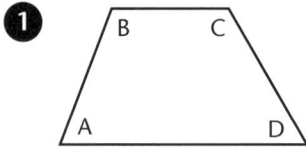

1

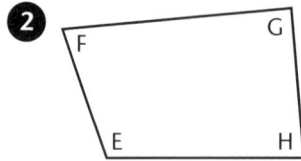

2

Which of the angles A–H are:

3 right angles ....

4 acute angles ....

5 obtuse angles ....

....

Use the intersections of the grid squares to help draw the shapes.

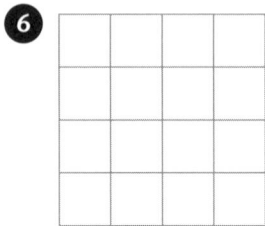

6

isosceles
triangle

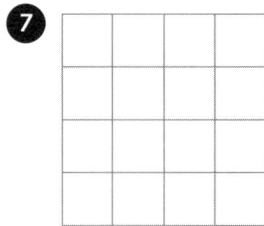

7

rhombus

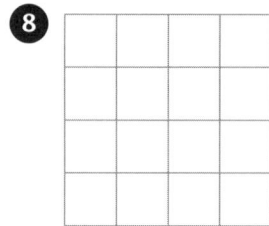

8

parallelogram

Draw the reflection in the mirror line.

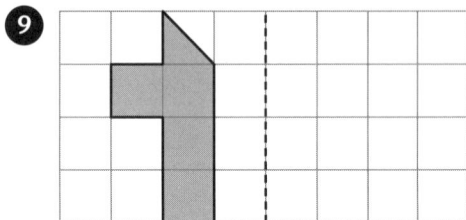

9

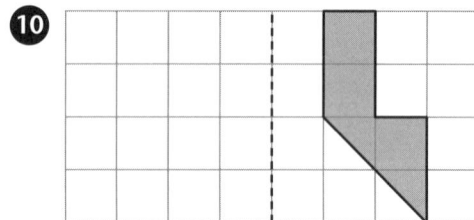

10

Plot the points and join up in the order given. Identify the shape.

11 (0, 2) (2, 6) (4, 5) (2, 1) (0, 2)

The shape is a ....

12 (4, 3) (6, 3) (3, 0) (3, 2) (4, 3)

The shape is a ....

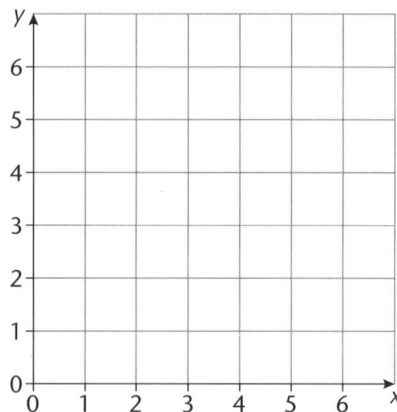

1. What is the sum of 74 and 59? ....

2. Find the area of a rectangle 20 cm long and 15 cm wide. ....

3. How many twelves make 84? ....

4. What number do you reach if you count back 8 from 5? ....

5. Write nine hundredths as a decimal fraction. ....

6. Find the difference between 115 and 48. ....

7. What is 0·35 litres in millilitres? ....

8. Write seven thousand and forty in figures. ....

9. What is the sixth multiple of 9? ....

10. Divide 24 by 100. ....

11. What is 400 more than 2835? ....

12. How many 5p coins make £2? ....

13. Round 4·52 to the nearest whole one. ....

14. Divide 3200 by 8. ....

15. Write 49 in Roman numerals. ....

16. What is the value of the 6 in 50·68? ....

17. Take seven tenths from 1. ....

18. Write 2700 g in kilograms. ....

19. How many months is 11 years? ....

20. What number is three times greater than 700? ....

21. Write LXXVI as an arabic number. ....

22. What number do you reach if you count on six fifties from 250? ....